THE BREAKING OF BREAD

A Short History of the Mass

BY

JOHN COVENTRY, S.J.

with sixty-three photographs

BY

JOHN GILLICK, S.J.

NEW YORK
SHEED & WARD
1950

FIRST PUBLISHED 1950
BY SHEED AND WARD, LTD.
110/111 FLEET STREET
LONDON, E.C.4

De licentia Superiorum Ordini;

NIHIL OBSTAT: GEORGIUS SMITH, S.T.D., PH.D.
CENSOR DEPUTATUS
IMPRIMATUR: E. MORROGH BERNARD
VIC. GEN.
WESTMONASTERII, DIE 24A JANUARY, 1950

CONTENTS

CHAPTER I

General Notions

THE PURPOSE OF THIS BOOK

EVEN THOSE of us who are quite familiar with the Mass have often taken it all rather for granted—understanding its meaning well enough, but vaguely thinking that the actual ceremonies and prayers have "been there always", or at any rate for a very long time. And it comes as a pleasant surprise and a matter of absorbing interest when we first see the Mass forming and taking shape. It becomes a living thing under our observation, growing and developing its latent germ of meaning, absorbing the ideas and forms of expression of different peoples at different times and then showing them forth in its own way. Suddenly we want to know the reason for everything that we have already long been used to. Why does the priest do this or say that? What would Mass have looked like in the fourth century? in the fourteenth? Why . . . ?

And those who are not used to being at Mass can none the less hardly fail to be interested in this most ancient piece of ritual which has wound its way for centuries in and out of European literature and art and architecture. We begin to realise that centuries of our history are here enshrined in a ceremony lasting half an hour—not in the glass cases of a museum nor even in the worn pages of a classic work which only our own mental vigour can bring back to life, but in a living tradition, a cultural and spiritualising force.

The history of the Mass's growth has been slowly unearthed by the patient labours of many scholars: and there is still—

there will always be—much to be discovered, to be corroborated, perhaps to be revised. But it seems a pity that information of such general and such absorbing interest should remain only in the learned volumes from which most of us have not the heart or the time to dig it out. This book unashamedly pilfers the achievements of these scholars in order to lay the gist of their discoveries, in as simple a form as possible, before the general public. The pundits will have to be lenient. Better to risk some inaccuracy of statement here and there than to avoid all possibility of error only by denying to the unprofessional reader even a glimpse at the bold and clear outlines of the picture, or by presenting that picture in so guarded and complicated a fashion as to destroy its clarity and meaning.

Father John Gillick's photographs will show the reader exactly what happens at a Low Mass today; the text will try to tell him how it all came about.

RITUAL

It would be a severe strain on us if every time we approached God we had to think out how to set about it. We would feel the responsibility appalling and the claim on our emotions too great, particularly at times when we did not feel very religious, but turned to prayer straight from the bustle of everyday life. One function of ritual, therefore, is to canalise our prayer, to insure against the ups and downs of our moods and the wayward vulgarities of fashion. A ritual that is formed by long tradition, and which enshrines the deepest truths of our religion in a setting worthy of their grandeur, carries us along on its tide; it leads and forms our prayer in a sacred mould rather than waiting upon any burst of personal inspiration. It is there already to hand, and we have only to enter into it, to take it up and try to make it personal, to make it our own. Pagan ritual itself expresses that need of human nature to lay upon society and tradition the awful responsibility of approaching God;

and yet it is haunted throughout by the fear of failing, by the superstition that some detail may be done wrong or overlooked and the god may be offended after all.

For a Catholic, believing that he comes to Mass to offer no earthly victim to God, but the sacrifice of His own divine Son, the sense of responsibility is magnified a hundredfold. Yet in the Mass any personal feeling of fearfulness is transformed into a sense of privilege. For this is a ritual guaranteed. Not only is its worth guaranteed by the very central act which invests it with greater awe than any pagan sacrifice could instil, but the ritual setting of that central act is guaranteed. The Mass is the central act of worship, the Liturgy, of the Church in which the Spirit of God lives and guides; Christ lives on in His Body, the Church, and gives Himself to the Father again through our hands and lips. It is the Spirit of God Himself who has moved throughout the centuries of our history and fashioned for us this liturgy, which therefore bears the weight not only of our beliefs but of that Christian history itself. There are other rites in Christendom besides the Western rite— Byzantine, Syrian, Coptic and the rest—and a work of this size can only afford passing reference to them, fascinating though they are.[1] They each reflect the growth of God's Church and the movement of His Spirit through other cultures and other lands. Our Western Mass enshrines and brings to us alive, as it were, the passage of Christ through the lands where our own civilisation, our own ways of thought and expression, were fostered and matured. But the various rites are only different settings of the same Eucharist: there is one Mass. There are varieties of detail and of atmosphere, but a central core of ritual that is common.

[1] Catholics sometimes ask whether they are " allowed " to go to a Mass performed in some rite other than the Latin. They are not merely allowed but encouraged to do so should any occasion offer of getting to know what the other rites are like—other Catholic rites, of course; they thereby fulfil their obligation of hearing Mass on a day when it is in force; and they may receive Holy Communion.

Ritual belongs more to public than to private worship, to the occasions when we pray as a people, as a family of families, conscious of our mutual interdependence and of a certain solidarity before God. But the Mass is more than the ritual of a people or of a culture: it is the worship of a spiritual and not of a merely social unity, which shares a common spiritual life—the supernatural life of grace which Our Lord came to live in His Church. It is the worship of the Body of Christ, which extends itself over all peoples and all cultures. A Catholic feels a great sense of exaltation in this realisation of one Mass, the same the world over, in which he shares; of one altar of God before which all differences of race or class evaporate. And just as he is sustained by the sense of *horizontal* solidarity, so he finds the realisation of *vertical* unity a great anchor, as he finds it a great mould and spiritualising power, for his prayer. This is the Mass which Augustine offered on the shores of Africa in the fourth century, as it is the Mass which Xavier carried in the sixteenth to the shores of Japan. Here are sentiments which the people of God have always expressed, words they have always used, above all a deed they have always done, charged ever with the same import and worth—the unending prayer of Christ in His Church, round which all other Christian prayer revolves.

And yet if there is one thing which even an elementary study of the history of the Mass makes quite clear it is that liturgy is a living and a growing thing; it is not in its nature to stick fast and ossify. It is hard to convey in words this impression one gets of development combined with age-old sameness and tradition: the impression must be drawn from first-hand study of the Mass's history, while one's words may even seem to conflict. One may say with one breath that the Spirit of God shapes the liturgy in His Church, and with the next imply some criticism of a development that has taken place. As always with the Church, as with the Incarnation itself which the Church continues, the divine and human are not laid side by side or one above the other; they are shot through each other, and no simple statement will ever explain their mutual relation; the human is divinised—and remains very human.

The principle that should govern our appreciation of the human setting for God's Gift is this: no age can grasp the *whole* of that Gift—Real Presence, Sacrifice and Sacrament. Man has enshrined God's Gift in the Mass; at different times, and without *denying* any of the rich content of the Mass, he has placed the emphasis on the aspect of it which appeals most to his needs or insight. Now it may be the meal of unity in Christ; now the life-giving Flesh and Blood; again, the sacrifice of praise. The emphasis may go to the sacramental Gift, or to the lesser gifts hoped for from the sacrifice. The thought of the Person present may dominate, or of His original action which is here re-presented. Now awe dominates, now homeliness. What matter? The *thing done*, the *Gift* itself, remains unchanged and contains all this and more. Hence we can neither look forward nor backward for the complete and perfect ritual for Mass; we must try to reach from old and new what most deepens our appreciation, grips us and helps us to make of the Mass the most perfect act of worship for our time.

Some devotees of liturgy almost speak as if the only good things in liturgy were the most ancient, as if the only right way of doing things were the earliest way known. It is not as simple as that. One may perhaps criticise this development and that as being less suitable than an older custom to express the central meaning of what is being done. But to refuse all change is to destroy the soul of liturgy, which has always lived by absorbing and drawing into the service of God the cultural outlook and habits of developing peoples. The Mass grew unceasingly in Europe till the Reformation, differences of practice in different countries, according to local custom, being quite general and fully expected and understood. But the extravagances of the

Reformers and the attempt to abolish the Mass itself caused a stiffening in the Church: everyone, as it were, was called within the fort to man the defences; the Church must hold on tight to what it had got; rigid conservatism became the order of the day of peril. Now that the peril has gone back to where it always was—outside and not inside the Christian family—there are signs that liturgy has begun to move again. No great changes are to be expected, nor are they desirable: the growth of liturgy has always been gradual and thoughtful, almost imperceptible. And now that travel is so much more rapid and more widespread, it is arguable that a far greater degree of uniformity, even in the smallest details, is desirable.

THE MEANING OF THE MASS

This short book is forced to be selective and to leave out many things it would be interesting to explore. Nothing is said about the history of the Mass vestments, practically nothing about the sacred vessels, the churches and their furniture and dispositions. Low Mass alone is examined directly and the ritual of High Mass referred to only by way of occasional illustration, so that its singing, its use of incense, its ceremonial and assistants are passed over. Then there is Pontifical (a bishop's) Mass, Holy Week Services . . . and all the rich variety of the liturgy.

But a few words must be said, however inadequate a few words must always be, about the meaning of the Mass, sacrifice and sacrament. For this meaning, all that has so far been said about ritual provides only the setting and framework; the remaining chapters of the book only give its expression and adornment.

Before thinking about the sacrifice of the Mass we should distinguish the inner, spiritual meaning of sacrifice—which may be called *real* sacrifice—from the outward expression of that deep religious attitude—which may be called *ritual* sacrifice. We are men, not disembodied spirits, and it is as natural for us to express outwardly our deepest religious ideas, as it is for us to bring our outward bodies into our prayers and serve God with word and gesture.

A *real* sacrifice is the effective submission of a man's heart and mind and will—his most inward and spiritual self—to God. A *ritual* sacrifice is the outward manifestation of that deep submission. Men of all ages have conducted ritual sacrifice, in an attempt to show forth that inward attitude: in particular, (1) they have tried to show God that they owe everything to Him by making the gesture of offering to Him (often by destroying the victim) what they prized most: their crops and herds, even human beings; and (2) they have tried by some similar gesture to make up for their sins, to re-establish a broken submission.

After sin, however, an effective sacrifice on man's part was impossible. Men were still bound, as God's "family", to worship Him, but could no longer re-establish, one-sidedly and by their own act, the broken relation to God. Man's sacrifices had not in themselves the power to remit sin; he could not make his submission effective. He could perhaps proffer, but no more. God must intervene.

Our Lord was God-man and therefore in Him human nature was of necessity submitted perfectly and effectively to God; in Him a real sacrifice was not only possible but resulted from His very nature. All His life on earth was the real sacrifice of a perfect human nature to God. But He chose to sum up that real sacrifice in a ritual sacrifice—His passion and death—offered for the whole of humanity, which God would accept as the means of extending *to us* the right-relation-to-God, the real sacrifice and submission, which always held good *in Christ*.

Thus Our Lord's ritual sacrifice (the expression of a real one) was the means chosen by God for our redemption. Christ offered Himself in the Last Supper; He consummated that sacrifice on the Cross; it was accepted by the Father in the

Resurrection and Ascension, so that for ever Our Lord endures in heaven as the accepted Victim for our sins, the source of grace and supernatural life (right relation to God) for all men.

But our redemption was not to be automatic. We are to be redeemed and graced as men, as free co-operating agents. The treasure is all there in the sacrifice of Christ, but we must lay hold of it; it must be poured out on us at our own bidding.

In the sacrifice of the Mass it is the Victim of Calvary who comes down on our altars at the words of consecration, at the bidding of the priest and people. Therefore it is the same sacrifice as that of the Cross, for the Victim is the same and, in so far as our priesthood is only a share in Christ's high-priesthood and headship of the human race, the Priest who offers it is the same. The manner of offering alone differs.

One might ask: why go on offering continually the same sacrifice? The answer is not only that man is at all times bound to worship God, but also that the Mass deploys the sacrifice of Calvary in time and space. On the Cross Christ died alone; we were not there and could not be there. The Mass is God's wonderful devising whereby, since we could not be on Calvary, Calvary is brought to us. In our Mass *we offer* to God His only Son, and thereby is put into our hands an act of worship transcending in every way anything that human nature could have planned. In our Mass *we are offered* to God with Christ, united to Him, with all our concerns and hopes and fears. *This* human nature, this twentieth century, with all its blemishes and needs, is offered to God in Christ. This people of London, of Birmingham, this village congregation, is drawn into the sacrifice of Christ.

The Mass is *our* sacrifice, our *real* sacrifice, for it is possible for us to make a real and effective submission to God only in so far as we are caught up into the sacrifice, the real submission, of Christ. In the Mass our right relation to God, as His sons, is more and more established.

Thus the Mass is sacrament[1] as well as sacrifice—not in two separate layers, but in mutual dependence. It is the Victim of Calvary, become the victim of our own altar, whom we receive in Holy Communion as a means of grace and of nourishment of the supernatural life of our souls, i.e. as a sacrament. Thus the sacrament draws its power and meaning from the sacrifice. And, conversely, the sacrifice is completed in the sacrament: for the whole purpose of the sacrifice is that we should be offered more effectively to God in union with His Son, and *so* nourish the life of grace in our souls—and how can we be more fully united to Our Lord than when we receive Him in Holy Communion, when we partake and communicate in the offering of our altar?

The Mass is the sacrifice of the Church, of the Body of Christ. He died alone on Calvary, but in and through the Mass His whole Body is, step by step, united to Him and offered with Him, and the sacrifice of the whole Christ becomes complete. That is the meaning of the Mass.

Public and Private Masses

Nowadays we are accustomed to regard Low Mass, said by a priest with one or two servers, as the regular and ordinary form of Mass, and to reserve for special occasions the celebration of Solemn High Mass, sung by a priest (or bishop, of course) assisted by deacon and subdeacon (usually other priests taking these roles), a Master of Ceremonies, acolytes, thurifer and choir. In most parishes the main Mass on a Sunday is an intermediary ceremonial, the *Missa cantata*, sung by a single priest without deacon or subdeacon. But in one sense High Mass should be regarded as the ordinary, or at any rate standard, type of the Mass.

[1] A Sacrament is an action of the Church (an outward action through her accredited members) directed by Christ to be a means of giving grace.

Only a rough picture can be given here, but if we go back to the origins we find we must distinguish three things: the public Eucharist of a Sunday or feast day, celebrated before and in the name of the whole people of a district (solemn Mass); the Eucharist celebrated on other days for a smaller group, perhaps for the dead of some family or society (semi-public Mass); the Eucharist offered by a priest as his own sacrifice, more or less by himself (private Mass). In the nature of things, the evidence for private Masses in the early centuries is less certain and less abundant, but as in the Old Testament we often find a sacrifice being offered by an individual in his own name, so in Christian times we find this idea persisting: the sacrifice of the New Covenant was to fulfil and perfect *all* the aspirations of both pagan and Jewish cult. We do not get much information about these private Masses until the formation of the monasteries, when the question of many priests living together without a " parish " would first arise.

The type *par excellence* of the Eucharist was from the beginning the bishop's solemn Mass. The earliest Christian use of the word " church "[1] (*ecclesia*) is for a gathering of people, not a building, and in the New Testament itself we hear of the Christians gathering in private houses for the celebration of the Eucharist by the apostles. Out of this grew the normal type of public Mass celebrated by the bishop with all his clergy, priests and deacons, grouped on either side of him in a semi-circle; the faithful beyond would be headed by the choir. It was probably usual for all the clergy to *face* the people during the lessons and chants at the beginning, and during the Offertory. And even during the formal prayers said by the celebrant in the name of the people—the *orationes* and the Canon itself—we find in early times that in some churches in the West the clergy faced the people, with the table of sacrifice between celebrant and con-

---

[1] Our actual word " church " derives ultimately from the Greek *kyriakon*, " The Lord's " (place, house); cf. the word " kirk ".

gregation.[1] The other grouping, with clergy and people all facing east and the celebrant leading the prayers and, so to speak, directing them, seems to have been more common; it was the only practice known in the East. By the early Middle Ages the whole of a priest's Mass was celebrated with the priest's back to the people, but at a pontifical Mass today the bishop still sits facing the people for the lessons, and only turns to the altar when he himself leads the prayer of the Church.

This arrangement of people and clergy could easily be managed in a private house and when public buildings, churches, began to be constructed for the purpose it dictated their shape; long before the persecution of the Church officially ended (313) there were many such churches, of different sizes, in a city like Rome, which is estimated to have had about thirty thousand Christians, or three per cent of the population, in the middle of the third century.

About such a solemn Mass there are two things particularly to note. The first is that all the early parts of the Mass, the lessons and chants, etc., were really no concern of the officiating bishop, the celebrant, who, except for the *orationes*, only began his own proper liturgy with the Eucharistic Prayer, when all the readings and preparations had been performed by the other clergy present; he would, however, preach the sermon. In fact it is not till about the eleventh century, at any rate in a public or semi-public Low Mass, that the celebrant read all of the Mass himself, including the chants and the Epistle. The second thing to note is that at a centre such as the bishop's church only he would celebrate the Eucharist on a solemn and public occasion and all the other priests of that church would assist at his Mass. This idea persists for a long time, and only well into the Middle Ages do we find our form of High Mass, sung by a priest with *only two* assistant clergy at the altar (and not all the clergy who

[1] It was an early custom to face east for the *orationes*, and the position of the building determined whether the celebrant faced the people during them or not. The earliest basilicas at Rome do not face east.

could be present), becoming the regular thing. From the same practice develops the Conventual Mass of cathedrals or monasteries, at which all the clergy of the chapter have to be present (in the stalls, not at the altar); and to it is allied the very early but quite different custom of *concelebration*, in which a number of priests say together the same Mass. This latter practice is quite usual in the Eastern liturgies, but only occurs now in the Roman rite at ordinations.

From the very earliest times, with the spread of the Church and its consequent organisation, we find growing up side by side with the bishop's solemn Mass the public Masses celebrated by priests in smaller places on the same pattern. From this grew our *Missa cantata*. As much of the solemnity as could be managed would be observed, and a single priest would be assisted by at least a deacon or acolyte (an ordained cleric), who would read some or all of the lessons, and by some form of choir.

A word about the Pope's Stational Mass, as much of the history of the Roman rite is bound up with it. In the sixth century Rome had been divided into seven ecclesiastical regions, each of which came into office by rote on the different days of the week. The " station " (a term borrowed from military language) was the celebration of Mass by the Pope in an appointed church in Rome. The clergy of the region on duty would go to the Lateran and escort the Pope in procession to the stational church, where he was awaited by the faithful of that church and all the clergy of the other regions who could manage to be there. The procession from the Lateran would be mounted on horseback if the distance was sufficiently great. Arriving at the church, the Pope went to a vestibule at the entrance of the church (*secretarium*), where he vested and where all arrangements were made with the choir and assistants; then followed his solemn entry into the church, preceded by lighted candles, and on reaching the altar he bowed to it, signed himself on the forehead and bowed to pray silently till the entrance chant (Introit) was finished; he then advanced to the altar and kissed it, before going to his *cathedra* while the lessons were sung. This ritual shows the most solemn form of beginning Mass, and to it the opening of our High or Low Mass is allied.

VARIOUS

Reference will have to be made occasionally to departments of the Western rite, customs existing elsewhere in Europe than at Rome, and it is difficult to avoid any complicated discussion of them and yet leave the reader with a sufficiently clear idea of what is meant. It would be quite wrong to think of all liturgical practices in the West as originating at Rome and being disseminated from there. This is only partly true at any time, and for many of the developments the boot is quite on the other foot. The exchange was mutual. All the regions of Europe developed their own local customs, and it is often rather a case of these being slowly adopted by a very conservative Rome than of the reverse process.[1] The Gallican rite was, strictly speaking, the customs proper to Gaul and Frankish lands before the reform of Charlemagne in the early ninth century. But it was not in fact abolished by him, and so one can use the term " Gallican " to cover roughly the customs of the lands which can now be described as in the area of France and Western Germany. That is how the term will be used here, to avoid complicating historical details. One particularly striking factor in the development of the Roman rite was that the influence of Eastern on Western liturgy came to Rome by way of the Gallican rite, and not directly. With the increasing spread over Europe of liturgical books produced at Rome, and the infiltration into Rome of Gallican practices, Western liturgy eventually settled down to a fairly uniform Gallico-Roman practice, which can be called the Roman rite. Many local customs, however, have

[1] This characteristic Roman conservatism proved a very salutary check on many extravagances.

survived, and the monastic Orders in particular have here and there preserved differences of usage from the Roman rite we now meet in all the churches of Western Catholic rite—i.e. all over the world.

Our modern liturgy preserves a strict distinction between the Ordinary of the Mass (the part that is always the same) and the Proper of the Mass (the prayers, readings and chants which vary according to the occasion being celebrated). But the ensuing chapters will show that variability was for long a matter of degree, and that practically every formula in the Mass which is now fixed and invariable only became so slowly, in the course of the development of the Roman rite and its spread over a wider and wider area as a uniform way of celebrating Mass.

The first liturgical language of the Eucharist was Greek, Christianity having arisen in the Eastern Provinces of the Roman Empire where Greek was the usual means of communication. At Rome itself the first Christians were Greeks and Hellenised Jews, and the Eucharist was celebrated there in Greek till the middle of the third century, when it was first translated into Latin; Greek continued to be used at Rome on occasion for at least another century. Hence the Latin prayers of the Mass do not, strictly speaking, go back to the earliest times, though they would in many cases have a direct ancestry in Greek prayers, which the evidence, though scanty, sometimes enables us to trace.

METHOD

The plan of this book will be to get the outline clear first, and then take in the details. Thus the main framework is briefly outlined in Chapter II; then this structure is examined more closely in Chapters III and IV, but still with the omission of many interesting details which might obscure the main picture before it had been sufficiently clarified. These details are collected in Chapter V in a final run-through, which presupposes all that has gone before. This method is adopted in the interests of clarity, and it is hoped that the reader will therefore excuse the occasional repetition which it involves. Finally there is added a Note on the Propers of the Roman Missal, which simply gives a selection from the wealth of information that might be produced, in order that some idea may be given of their composition.

As a result of this method it will be found that the first four chapters need to be read straight through, but that Chapter V is more a matter for piecemeal study, with one's eye on the text of the prayers; its details are meant to enrich and heighten a picture whose meaning is already clear.

CHAPTER II

Main Outline

THE FIRST thing to realise about the Mass is that the service we now know was once two distinct services, which were held quite separately and, though they began to be joined together to form one in the second century, can still be found in separation from each other as late as A.D. 500.[1] The first of these was devoted to prayer in common and to instruction; the second is the Eucharist proper.

The instruction-and-prayer service is often called the MASS OF THE CATECHUMENS, because when the two services were held as one the catechumens (those under instruction but not yet baptised) and any Jewish or pagan visitors who might be present had all to leave the church before the Eucharist began. The Eucharist is the Sacrifice and Sacrament of the faithful, and only those who could receive Communion were allowed to be present at it. The Mass of the Catechumens as we now know it has two chief parts: the *Entrance Rite* and the instruction-and-prayer rite. Of these the second is the older, the Entrance Rite being added after the Mass of the Catechumens and the Eucharist had been joined together, as an introduction to the whole Mass.

For purposes of brevity we may refer to the instruction-and-prayer rite as the *Synaxis*.[2] This name, one of the oldest in use

---

[1] People at this date would still attend the Synaxis in one church and the Eucharist in another, or would hold the Synaxis in separate groups in the same church, with a different language being used in each group.

[2] The word " Synaxis " was also used quite commonly for the whole Mass, and when taken over into Latin came eventually to be a name for Holy Communion.

among Christians, means simply " gathering " or " assembly "
and reminds us of the Jewish Synagogue—a name which
comes from the same Greek word. There is point in this re-
minder, for the Synaxis was nothing more nor less than a
continuation in Christian circles of the practice of the
Synagogue, modified of course by a Christian content and
character. The need for instructing the faithful in their
religion and of making them familiar with the sacred Scriptures, and the need felt by any religious body of meeting
together to say prayers of a quite general character, existed
under the Old Covenant as under the New, and it was natural
for the first Christians to satisfy these needs more or less in
their traditional way.

The EUCHARIST itself, instituted by Our Lord at the Last
Supper, always had the character of a meal—a sacrificial meal,
as was the Paschal Supper itself. In the earliest days of the
Church it would often be celebrated after a meal which the
faithful took together in common (called the Agapé or love-
feast) as a sign of their union and mutual love, as a way of
helping the poorer among them, and in remembrance of the
many times Our Lord had sat at table with His disciples both
before and after the Resurrection. Even the ordinary meals of
a Jewish household had a religious character (to the Jews
religion was very much a part of daily life), and at these the
father of the family would pronounce blessings over the food
and wine according to prescribed formulas. Such meals ended
with a special Cup of Blessing (very like our grace after meals),
and it was this Cup of Blessing after a religious meal shared
by the Christian family that the early Christians often made
the occasion for celebrating the Eucharist, as Our Lord
Himself had done.[1] Or they would celebrate it after the Synaxis,
or even by itself.

The Eucharist has from the beginning four distinct parts:

[1] See p. 36, and Luke xxii. 20; 1 Cor. xi. 25.

the Offertory, the Eucharistic (which means " thanksgiving ")
Prayer, the Breaking, and the Communion. To these four parts
a Conclusion was later added as epilogue, much as the Entrance
Rite had been prefixed as introduction to the whole Mass. The
Offertory was a bringing by the faithful of gifts of bread and
wine which were to be consecrated in the sacrifice. When the
Eucharist was held after an Agapé, part of the gifts brought by
the faithful would be used for this purpose; otherwise gifts of
bread and wine were specially brought by them for the Eucharist. Thus it was clear from the beginning that the sacrifice to be
offered was *their* offering, the offering of all present. The
changing of their own gifts into the Body and Blood of Christ
symbolised the fact that in the Eucharist they themselves and
all the concerns of their daily lives were to be transformed into
Christ and quickened by the new life He came to give. The
Eucharistic Prayer was then said over the gifts by the officiating
bishop or priest, and during it occurred the words of consecration. The *Breaking* then followed, i.e., the breaking up of the
consecrated Bread so that it could be distributed among those
present. And finally the *Communion* itself was the distribution
of the consecrated Bread and Wine. The last three parts of the
Eucharist correspond exactly to what we know Our Lord did
at the Last Supper—" He took bread and blessed it[1] (Eucharistic Prayer), and broke (Breaking), and gave to his disciples
(Communion), saying . . . "[2] We shall note before passing
on that only one of these four parts of the Eucharist requires
of its nature that anything be *said*, the Eucharistic Prayer;
in the other three parts it is primarily what is *done* that is
significant.

[1] Or, as St. Luke (xxii. 19) and St. Paul (1. Cor. xi. 24) say, " and gave
thanks "—the Greek being " eucharistesas ". See p. 36.
[2] Matt. xxvi. 26; Mark xiv. 22.

We have, then, the following divisions of the Mass:

MASS
    Mass of the Catechumens
        Entrance Rite
        Synaxis

    Eucharist
        Offertory
        Eucharistic Prayer
        Breaking
        Communion
        Conclusion

CHAPTER III

The Mass of the Catechumens

ENTRANCE RITE

THIS RITE corresponds to all that happens in our Mass from the beginning to the Collect[1] inclusive, i.e. till just before the priest reads the Epistle. As has been said, none of this part of the Mass goes back to the very earliest times, but developed as an introduction to the Mass after the Synaxis and the Eucharist had been joined together to form one rite. The Mass has been well compared to a great temple, of which the Eucharist forms the central part and to which the Synaxis was added as a large outer court; then, later, further vestibules and porches were added—at both ends of the Mass—as a sort of outer adornment. Thus the first and the last parts of the Mass are the latest of all to develop[2] and, forming as they do an introduction and epilogue, can only be properly understood when one has traced the growth of the central part of which they were the outer adornments.

Within this Entrance Rite itself there is an earlier and a later layer of development, so it will be better to start with what comes first in the course of history rather than with the beginning of the Mass as we now know it.

Nowadays when a priest walks on to the altar from the sacristy we do not get the impression of a full ceremonial

---

[1] For the name " Collect " see p. 71.

[2] When dealing with liturgy one regards anything before the fourth century as primitive, and anything up to the fifth and sixth centuries, when we begin to get really full information, as early; developments during the Middle Ages are late, and any changes made since the fifteenth century are recent.

entrance of the celebrant and ministers. At High Mass, when
there is a longer procession, preceded by the thurifer and
acolytes with lighted candles, and the priest is preceded by
subdeacon and deacon, this idea is more fully conveyed; more
elaborate still is the entrance of a bishop, for in this case the
ministers are all ready at the altar and the bishop comes right
up the aisle of the church, led by acolytes, while the choir sing
the *Ecce sacerdos*. It is this latter picture which represents most
fully the Entrance Rite. At the Pope's Stational Mass, or when
a bishop went to some nearby church to celebrate Mass, the
actual arrival of the visiting clergy at the church was a ceremonial event: the celebrant and his ministers would gather at
their own centre and then go in procession to the church in
question, on horseback if it was some distance away. They
would then shed their travelling garments in some outer vestibule, put on their vestments and enter the church in procession;
if the church had no such outer vestibule they would vest on
reaching the altar—and a bishop still vests at the altar and not
in the sacristy. In either case their arrival in the church was
greeted by the congregation.

We now come to a new factor—the introduction of music
into the liturgy. The whole Entrance Rite as just described
belonged, of course, to the days when the Church was no longer
persecuted and could assemble openly and with some celebration; i.e. this rite could not begin to take its full form till the
late third century, and it is from soon after this time that we
learn of the introduction of music into the liturgy of the Mass.
Christians had had their hymns from the beginning—St. Paul
mentions them[1] and even quotes them[2]—but the addition of
music to the Mass itself belongs to a time when this had begun
to be a public and festive ritual, when the great basilicas could
be built in Rome, and when all the arts began to be laid at the

[1] e.g. Eph. v. 19.
[2] e.g. Eph. v. 14; 1 Tim. iii. 16.

service of the Mass. The **Introit**[1] was the song with which
the choir greeted the arrival of the celebrant and his ministers
and accompanied their procession up the church. In the earliest
Mass-texts it is always a psalm and varies with the occasion.
Now it has been cut down to its barest minimum because the
entrance procession no longer takes place in its full splendour,
but originally a whole psalm would be sung (which could easily
be needed if the ministers were going to vest in the sanctuary),
or as much of it as was necessary until the celebrant gave a sign
for the end or went up to the altar and greeted it with a **kiss**
—a sign of reverence for the table on which the Body of Our
Lord is going to lie. This greeting now takes place after the
prayers at the foot of the altar.

This is a good place to notice a certain pattern which keeps
recurring during the Mass. The Entrance, a procession, is
accompanied by a psalmody (the Introit) and concludes with
a formal prayer (the **Collect**). In such a formal prayer (*oratio*)
the priest speaks to God in the name of the whole people present:
he prays to God " through Christ our Lord ", a formula which
forms the conclusion of the prayer; the whole people (originally
—now only the server) answer *Amen*, the prayer is preceded by
a greeting (*Dominus vobiscum*[2]) answered by the people (*Et cum
spiritu tuo*[3]), and by a call to prayer (*Oremus*[4]). Thus the prayer
forms the climax of the Entrance Rite, a conclusion to which
the rest has led up. Now this pattern—a procession of some
sort, accompanied by singing and concluded by a formal *oratio*
—occurs at two other places in the Mass, and each time the
prayer is the climax of a clearly definable section of the Mass.
The second time this pattern occurs is at the Offertory: the
procession is that of the faithful bringing up their gifts to the
altar, accompanied by the Offertory chant, the whole Offertory

---

[1] The word means " Entrance ".
[2] " The Lord be with you (plural)."
[3] "And with thy spirit."
[4] " Let us pray."

concluding with the *oratio super oblata*,[1] now called the Secret. The third time the pattern occurs is at the Communion: the procession is that of the faithful coming to receive Communion, while the choir sing the Communion chant, and the whole rite of Communion is concluded by a formal prayer, the Post-Communion. All these parts of the Mass will receive explanation in their place, but we may note here the recurrence of the same pattern and the beginning of an idea which was to play a great part in the development of the Mass—that of " covering " with singing some action, which had previously been carried out in silence. As will be seen later, a great many prayers were introduced to " cover ", to be said during, some action, thus giving expression to the thoughts which were in people's minds while they performed the actions. We must not let these developments obscure the fact that the actions are in these cases older than the words and have a meaning of their own: they symbolise something. In the Roman rite the three chants referred to were all introduced at about the same time, in the course of the fourth century or soon after. They are all, like the corresponding prayers—Collect, Secret and Post-Communion —variable with the day and the occasion and so are found in the Proper of the Mass.[2]

Now it will have occurred to anyone at all familiar with the Mass that in our Mass, quite apart from anything that may have been added before the Introit, there are other things which come in between Introit and Collect, viz. the *Kyrie* and *Gloria*. These do not fit so easily into the scheme of the Entrance Rite, and we must remind ourselves of the fact that the ritual of the Mass grew up out of various elements in the course of time and was not planned in all its details by anyone beforehand. The three **Kyrie eleisons,** followed by three *Christe eleisons* and then three more *Kyries* are the only bit of Greek in our

---

[1] " Prayer over the gifts (offerings)."   For the name " Secret " see p. 34.
[2] See p. 14 and Appendix I.

Mass,[1] but they are not, as is sometimes supposed, a survival in our Latin Mass from the time when it was said in Greek even at Rome. This repeated prayer was an acclamation by the people, or by clergy and people together, and only later came to be said all through by the priest. It was borrowed by Rome from the litanies (lists of petitions) which had come to play an important part in the Eastern rites, and we meet it also in our own litanies, e.g. the Litany of the Saints on Holy Saturday. The *Kyrie* only came into the Roman Mass in the fifth or early sixth century after the Entrance Rite had taken definite shape.

The **Gloria** is a very early Christian hymn, beginning with the hymn of the angels at Bethlehem;[2] it was not composed for the Mass but rather for occasions of very special celebration when we would use the *Te Deum*.[3] Outside Rome there are signs of its introduction into the Mass on very festive occasions earlier than at Rome, where it appears in the early sixth century, and then only for the greater feasts. It is now said (and sung) at nearly all Masses, excluding only those for the dead, vigils and other days of penitential character, e.g. in Lent and Advent. It was always, like the *Kyrie*, the people's hymn and not the priest's, though he intoned the first words.

All that comes before the Introit is of considerably later growth than the parts so far considered. That people should prepare for Mass by private prayers was, of course, an idea always current, but we first find these prayers of preparation taking definite form in the monasteries: there the prayers were modelled on parts of the Divine Office, and the Preparation for Mass became in some places almost a part of the daily Office,

---

[1] They mean " Lord have mercy (on us) " and " Christ have mercy (on us) " respectively. " Christ " is, of course, a Greek word meaning " The Anointed (One) " (always preceded by the definite article in Greek) and was the customary translation of the Jewish word " Messiah ".

[2] Luke ii. 14.

[3] A hymn attributed to St. Ambrose (fourth century), which is sung at Matins in the Divine Office and is also used for solemn occasions of thanksgiving.

forming a separate section of it.[1] The prayers of preparation are largely made up of the psalm (xlii[2]) **Judica me Deus** (" Judge me, O God, . . . "), with versicles taken from other psalms, and the **Confession** of sins and form of **Absolution** in use in the Divine Office.[3] The precise prayers now said at the beginning of Mass began taking shape in the tenth century in Europe, when they would either be said before Mass or on the way to the altar, and eventually became a regular part of the Mass itself and were begun at the foot of the altar. They express the feelings of unworthiness and the sense of sinfulness which are the best dispositions for priest and people in approaching this holy sacrifice.

SYNAXIS

This, it will be remembered, is the name we are using for the instruction-and-prayer rite which developed out of the practice of the Jewish synagogue, and was for long held quite separately from the Eucharist. It corresponds to all in our Mass from the Epistle to the *Credo*.

We read of Our Lord going into the synagogue at Nazareth, where the book of Isaiah the prophet was handed to Him, and that after reading some of the text He preached a sermon on it.[4] So, too, St. Paul, in the synagogue at Antioch, " after the reading of the law and the prophets " was asked to " make a word of exhortation to the people ".[5] We learn from other sources that the readings from the Bible in the synagogue were inter-

---

[1] In the Missal on certain penitential days, e.g. Ash Wednesday, is the note *dicta nona* (" When None has been said "). The Mass was inserted in the day's Office, so that on Sundays and feasts it followed Terce; on ordinary weekdays, Sext; on penitential weekdays, None. These " Hours " were recited at the time corresponding to their name—Terce (the third hour, i.e. after dawn) at 9 a.m., Sext at midday, None at 3 p.m. The time of Mass eventually got fixed (probably late ninth century) and the Hours were then crowded in before it. Holy Saturday Mass ends with Vespers.

[2] All references to the psalms will use the Vulgate numbering.

[3] e.g. every day at Compline.

[4] Luke iv. 16–20.

[5] Acts xiii. 15.

spersed with psalm-singing and that the people said prayers together in common before they went away.[1] These are just the elements which we find in the Christian Synaxis—readings from the Bible (**Epistle** and **Gospel**) interspersed with psalmody (**Gradual,** etc.) and the sermon. The synagogue readings consisted of two lessons (or " lections "), the first taken from the " Law " (the first five books of the Bible) and the second from the " Prophets " (the remaining books). The passages from the Law were arranged in a cycle to ensure that the whole of it was read every three years, but the passages from the Prophets were chosen more at random; Our Lord may have chosen the part He wanted from Isaiah that day at Nazareth, or He may have found the place marked. The number of lessons read by the Christians in their Synaxis varied, but was quite generally three for some time—the first from the Old Testament, the last from the four Gospels, and the middle one from the rest of the New Testament (Epistles, Acts and Apocalypse). We still have three lessons on certain days—e.g. Wednesday in Holy Week and Good Friday—and on some of the Ember Days even more, but the Roman rite settled down at an early stage to two. The first has come to be called the Epistle (though it is announced in Latin simply as a *lectio*) because it is mostly taken from the Epistles, though many " epistles " are from the Old Testament, the Acts or the Apocalypse; the second is the Gospel.

As the whole purpose of these readings was to instruct the faithful and make them familiar with Scripture, it is not surprising that from the earliest times they were read in different languages at the Synaxis, and sometimes in more than one language in the same church if the congregation was mixed. This practice is continued when the priest now reads them from the pulpit in our own language.

[1] The same arrangement occurs in the Divine Office, e.g. at the end of the Little Hours—lesson, psalm-versicles, prayer.

The psalmody between the Epistle and Gospel (Gradual, etc.), read by the priest but also chanted by the choir at a sung Mass, is now a very cut-down version of what it originally was. There was a general tendency in the Roman rite towards such abbreviation after the Synaxis and Eucharist had been joined together, and the other chants were cut down in the same way. This tendency was much assisted by the development and embellishment of the music of the chant; for, when chants were meant to accompany some action, fewer and fewer verses would be needed the more intricate the chant became.[1]

After the lessons came the homily or **Sermon** which it was primarily the bishop's function to deliver and which usually took the form of an explanatory commentary on the lessons of the day. From this practice arose the great commentaries or series of homilies on Scripture written by the Fathers of the Church; a part of one of these is said every day in the Divine Office. The general custom of preaching a Sunday sermon on the Gospel of the day also continues this tradition.

We remarked above that in the synagogue the sermon was followed by general prayers. This practice, too, was adopted in the Christian Synaxis, though with the joining of Synaxis and Eucharist these prayers dropped out from their old place and in their old form, at least in the Roman rite, except in so far as the Secret can be considered a survival of them.[2] At first the prayers would be composed by the celebrating bishop at his own discretion. But soon they came to take on a very definite form, suitable to the common prayers of the Church for all her interests, for the different classes of people she comprised, for preservation from sickness and other dangers, for her enemies and all those who were not Christians. Each separate prayer was preceded by a Call to Prayer of a more elaborate kind than

[1] See p. 66.
[2] See p. 88.

the simple *Oremus*,[1] and each was, like our Collect, directed to God, asking the particular favour from Him " through Christ our Lord ", the people all answering *Amen*. Any who have attended Holy Week services will already have recognised the Intercessory Prayers which we still use on Good Friday and now on that day alone.[2]

In fact the Good Friday service in its early part is a descendant of the old Synaxis. It begins abruptly with a lesson, as the Synaxis would probably have begun when held by itself and when the Entrance Rite had not yet been prefixed to it; the lesson is from the Old Testament and is followed by chant; then, after the Collect, comes another lesson, more psalmody, the Gospel; and then the ministers go straight on to the Intercessory Prayers.[3] Early in the series of these prayers in the Synaxis would come a prayer for the catechumens, after which they would be given a formal dismissal by the deacon[4] and would go out. Even when the Synaxis was held by itself they were not present at the Intercessory Prayers, for these are the prayers of the faithful, of the Church—family prayers. We shall see that, though these prayers dropped out of the Roman Mass at this point (they may still have occurred in all public Masses in the early fifth century), they reappear in a different form later on.[5]

The **Creed** was not introduced into the Mass at Rome until the eleventh century, though in other parts of Europe it begins

[1] The summons to prayer, made by the deacon, took the form: *Oremus. Flectamus genua. Levate. Oremus dilectissimi pro* . . . (" Let us pray. Let us bend the knee. Arise. Let us pray, dearly beloved, for . . . ").

[2] The multiplication of Collects on Ember Days, each preceded by *Oremus. Flectamus genua. Levate* is a further vestige of the Intercessory Prayers, but not in their full form.

[3] The insertion of the Collect is probably by analogy with the form of the Mass at this point, but it will be noted that there are other old survivals: no title to the " Epistle "; no *Munda cor meum*, etc.; no *Dominus vobiscum* . . . *Sequentia* . . .; the Gospel read at the epistle side by the celebrant; no kiss of the book, nor *Laus tibi Christe*.

[4] No trace of this dismissal is left in our Mass, but compare the deacon's dismissal *Ite Missa est* at the end of the Eucharist.

[5] See p. 42.

appearing in the sixth and earlier still in the East. Even then, though it comes into every Mass in other rites, its use at Rome was restricted to Sundays and greater feasts. Elsewhere it was for long *said* by the *people* and formed their response to the teaching given them in the lessons and the sermon. It came into the Mass, of course, long after the practice of dismissing the catechumens had been given up, for, when this was still in force, it is not likely that they would have been allowed to join in the Church's profession of faith.

CHAPTER IV

The Eucharist

OFFERTORY

IN THE very earliest days there would have been no special ritual connected with the material used for the Eucharist. This was simply a part of the gifts given by the faithful to the Church, not only for the Eucharist but also for the maintenance of the clergy and the poorer brethren. When the Eucharist was celebrated after an Agapé the bread and wine used for the Eucharist would be a part of that brought as gifts for the common feast. Such gifts would not necessarily be all in kind. The early Church connected the support of the poor and of their bishop and priests very closely with the Eucharist and the common table, and thus it came about that it was the role of the deacons, who had from the first been appointed to look after the poor,[1] to take charge of the reception of the offerings when this took ritual shape as part of the Eucharist. Even when the Offertory came to be a ritual part of the Mass, not all the bread and wine offered by the faithful would be consecrated, some being set aside for the poor and the clergy. Nor would all the gifts brought at the Offertory be bread and wine, but often other foodstuffs, oil, gold and silver plate for the sacred vessels, etc. So our present practice of receiving the gifts of the faithful at the Offertory in the form of money is in a real way a continuation of the most ancient practice. The custom of the faithful providing the bread and wine which was to be consecrated and

[1] Acts vi. 1–6.

afterwards received in Holy Communion was of great significance[1] and lasted for long, but it gradually went out of use, partly in the interests of efficiency and simplicity, partly to ensure that the bread and wine used were of a quality worthy of the Mass. With the introduction of unleavened bread into the Roman rite in the ninth century—partly on the ground that Our Lord had used unleavened bread at the Last Supper—the faithful, whose bread was the ordinary leavened bread, could no longer provide it, and it became more and more the privilege of religious Orders to prepare the hosts for use in the Mass.

Another reason why there was no particular ritual connected with the Offertory in the earliest days was the conscious desire of the Christians to make their offering different from the customary pagan sacrifices. But in the second century, in the face of heretics who declared matter to be evil and who exaggerated the spiritual nature of the Church even to the point of denying the reality of Our Lord's human nature, more emphasis began to be laid on the material gifts of the faithful.

Many of the oldest Roman prayers over the gifts (Secrets) bring out the idea that in the Mass a holy exchange (*commercium*) takes place: we bring earthly and material gifts to the Church and receive back spiritual and heavenly gifts. The idea of transforming the earthly into the spiritual is, of course, fundamental to Christianity—to the Incarnation itself, to the Church, to all the Sacraments, and to the Eucharist in particular.

We do not learn any details about the Offertory until the fourth century; it would have been done in various ways in different places. The Roman custom seems at first to have been that the deacons went among the congregation collecting their gifts and then brought them up to tables or receptacles standing beside the altar: the Emperor Constantine is reported to have given to the Lateran basilica (about A.D. 320) seven such tables of gold and silver, to correspond to the seven original deacons.

[1] See p. 18.

The custom of the faithful coming up in procession with their gifts is found in France as late as the sixteenth century, the priest in some places receiving the gifts of the faithful at the epistle side of the altar and giving a blessing to each. A trace of this practice can still be seen in the ordination of a priest, when the ordinand brings a lighted candle at the Offertory to the bishop seated at his faldstool, or in the lighted candles and small barrels of wine with two loaves similarly offered by a bishop at his consecration. An actual procession of the faithful with the gifts began to be restricted, even where it was customary, to more festive occasions, and eventually to a few great feasts, before it dropped out altogether; but about A.D. 1000 it was still quite a common practice on Sundays.

Nothing so far has been said about any *words* used during the Offertory, which was first and foremost something *done*. The first thing in the nature of a prayer to be connected with it was the **Offertory chant** which was introduced about the same time as the Introit and Communion chant (or perhaps a little later) and was sung by the choir while the action of bringing up the gifts proceeded;[1] like the other chants, it was originally a whole psalm, but dwindled in the course of time, with the lapse of the Offertory procession and the embellishment of the chant (causing fewer words to last the required time), so that we now have only a single verse. A longer Offertory chant has survived in Masses for the dead, because in these the bringing up of gifts (for Masses for the soul of the dead person) by the family or guild concerned lasted much longer. This chant is still sung by the choir at a High Mass.

At Mass now the priest himself sets everything ready for the sacrifice during the Offertory, assisted by the server or ministers; the server's bringing up of the wine represents the old bringing up of gifts. The prayers the priest says during this preparation, up to the *Orate fratres* (" Pray, brethren, that my

[1] See p. 22.

sacrifice and yours . . . ”), are all of much later origin than the Offertory chant and will be dealt with in detail later. We here meet again, as with the prayers at the foot of the altar, the phenomenon of prayers which began as private devotions, eventually finding their way in fixed forms into the Ordinary of the Mass. In the various Mass-books of the Middle Ages there is a great variety of prayers to be found at this place, sometimes as alternatives for the priest to choose from, sometimes as mere suggestions of the sort of prayer he might like to use during the Offertory procession or his own preparation of the sacrifice—all expressing the thoughts which would be occupying his mind at this time. Two very notable characteristics of these prayers are that they are said *in silence* by the priest, and that some of them are in the first person singular, e.g. the *Suscipe sancte Pater* and *Suscipe sancta Trinitas* (“ Receive, O holy Father . . . ”, and “ Receive, O holy Trinity . . . ”): both these traits show their origin in private devotion, and that they are really the priest’s own prayers and not, like the main and oldest prayers of the Mass, said by him in the name of and on behalf of the whole people. The particular prayers that are now said at this place in the Roman rite are simply some from among this number, all being forms of prayer which had long been traditional but whose exact wording only slowly became generally established.

Towards the end of the Offertory the priest **washes his hands**—or, rather, the tips of his fingers. One might have expected this action to have had a practical rather than a symbolical origin, in that the priest’s hands might have become soiled in the course of receiving the various gifts of the faithful. But ritual hand-washing is an exceedingly ancient usage, going back even before the development of the Offertory ritual, and seems always to have had a symbolical value. The Jews themselves made much use of purificatory washing in their ceremonies and ritual meals as a sign of the purity of heart and intention they wished to have in approaching a religious ritual. So in the Mass it looks forward as much as back and is part of the priest's preparation of himself for the Eucharist. The use of the psalm (xxv) *Lavabo* (" I will wash my hands among the innocent . . . ") in this place (of which the wording is in the first person singular) comes from the Middle Ages and originates, like the other Offertory prayers, in the priest's private devotion. Thus, as with the Offertory as a whole, the action is of very ancient usage, but the accompanying words more modern.

Whereas all these prayers at the Offertory, up to the *Orate fratres*, were always said in silence by the priest, the old Roman liturgy had known only one prayer, the *oratio super oblata*,[1] said *aloud* by the priest in the name of the people; it is the prayer now called the **Secret,** in which the priest gathers together all that the people intend by their offering of gifts into one formal prayer. Like the Collect and Post-Communion, it brings to a formal end one clear-cut section of the Mass which has been accompanied by a chant; like them, it was from the beginning variable according to the feast or occasion being celebrated. There is no real certainty about the name " Secret " (*oratio secreta*) for this prayer over the gifts, but it seems that the most obvious explanation is the right one—that it was so called when, and because, it had come to be said inaudibly by the priest. It is a Gallican name, and we first hear of this prayer being said silently in Gallican lands in the eighth century. As to *why* the prayer was said silently one can only say that it was part of the general trend to silent prayer which began about then and resulted in the whole Eucharistic Prayer being said silently, as is now the case.

We have seen one explanation for the introduction of silent prayer into the Mass, namely the origin of some Mass prayers in private devotion. But this can provide no explanation for the

---

[1] " Prayer over the gifts (offerings)."

inaudible Secret, a formal *oratio* said by the priest in the name of the whole congregation; still less can it explain the silent Canon, the central and most solemn of all the " formal prayers " of the Mass.

No full explanation of the silent Canon has ever been given. Some have invoked the special regulation of secrecy about the mysteries of the Eucharist, whereby the faithful were forbidden to divulge to non-Christians what was said and done there. But this regulation arose and died within too short, and at too early, a time to explain the silent Canon; and, besides, only the faithful were then present at the Canon. One can appeal to the general desire to express and to ensure by outward forms the reverence in which the Eucharist had always been held—a tendency which accounts for many regulations about Mass and the giving of Holy Communion—and to an age when awe was emphasised rather than homeliness and familiarity.[1] But such a general trend does not fully account by itself for so great a change as this. Secrecy came from the East to Gallican lands and thence to Rome, where the Canon became silent in the ninth century, and one may perhaps recall the general tendency of the Eastern Christians towards mystery or, as we might say of some of the more extreme manifestations of this trend, mystification. But even this factor does not solve our problem, because the Eastern rites do not in fact say the Canon inaudibly.

THE EUCHARISTIC PRAYER

This covers all from the beginning of the Preface till the *Amen* before the *Pater Noster*. It may cause some surprise to see all this part of the Mass described as " a " prayer; it seems to be many prayers. But in fact its original form was that of a single prayer, formally begun by the officiating bishop or priest with a Call to Prayer, and then proclaimed aloud by him for all to

[1] See pp. 5, 46-7.

hear, with the people together giving their assent to the Prayer by the concluding *Amen*. It is only the later insertions into the original form that have given it the appearance of many prayers instead of one, instead of *the* Prayer par excellence of the Eucharist.[1]

Our Lord Himself instituted the Eucharist (the Christian Thanksgiving) during the Last Supper. He did so on the occasion of the blessings prescribed for that supper, the Jewish form of blessing being a prayer of thanksgiving to God for the bread or wine being blessed—we have already noted that the evangelists use indifferently the phrases " He blessed " and " He gave thanks ",[2] the two meaning the same thing to them. Thus Our Lord as it were inserted into the form of thanksgiving-blessing, traditional at this supper, His own words, " This is My Body . . . "

From the earliest times that we have any information about the central prayer of the Eucharist we find that it is a prayer of this precise form—the form of the Jewish thanksgiving-blessing with an account of what Our Lord did and said inserted into it. At first, though this form of the Eucharistic Prayer would remain the same, the exact wording of it would be left to the bishop: it was his ceremonial prayer, the prayer which he as representative of all his people said, the thanksgiving he made, over the bread and wine, and with which he consecrated them into the Body and Blood of Christ. Very soon, however, the exact wording of the Prayer became fixed in various localities and we thus get the Eucharistic Prayers of the different rites—all closely resembling each other in their general form and content, but with differences of wording, different ideas developed here and there. The later insertions into the Eucharistic Prayer are rather additions to a traditional form than changes which radically alter the character of the Prayer.

[1] This part of the Mass was often called simply *prex*, The Prayer.
[2] See p. 18.

This traditional form of the Eucharistic Prayer is as follows. It opens with a **Dialogue** between celebrant and people, which serves as a more elaborate Call to Prayer than that found in other parts of the Mass. This dialogue is itself a feature of the Jewish thanksgiving-blessing. First comes the *Dominus vobiscum* (" The Lord be with you ") and the people's answer, *Et cum spiritu tuo* ("And with thy spirit "), which introduces all the formal *orationes* of the Mass;[1] it is a Jewish form of greeting and was used by the angel Gabriel to Our Lady;[2] its use is extended to many other parts of the Mass, but it always signalises that something particularly important is going to happen;[3] by it the celebrant, so to speak, establishes contact with the people so that all together may enter on the prayer in question. Next comes *Sursum corda* (" Lift up your hearts "[4]), with the reply, *Habemus ad Dominum* (" We have them (lifted up) to the Lord "), which performs the same function of a call to prayer as the more simple *Oremus* that occurs elsewhere. Then, after *Gratias agamus Domino Deo nostro* (" Let us give thanks to the Lord our God "), with its reply *Dignum et iustum est* (" It is meet and just "), the Eucharistic Prayer begins with *Vere dignum . . . gratias agere* (" It is truly meet and just for us . . . to give thanks . . . ").

The thanksgiving ("eucharistic ") character of the Prayer is emphasised by these opening phrases.[5] The traditional form of the Prayer *either* began with a long and invariable list of thanksgivings, which included all that the Church wanted to thank God for; *or*, as at Rome, instead of including all the thanksgivings every time, had a series of opening formulas each of which stressed the particular dispensation of God's goodness which it was appropriate to emphasise according to the time of

[1] For the call to prayer before the Secret, see p. 88.
[2] Luke i. 28.
[3] e.g. it occurs before the Gospel but not before the Epistle.
[4] Literally " up with (your) hearts ".
[5] The actual phrase " meet and just . . . *to give thanks* " is lost only in the Preface of the Apostles.

year or occasion—the Nativity, Easter, Pentecost, feasts of
Apostles, etc. Thus we get our **Prefaces**. The fact that this
part of the Mass was variable, and the introduction of the picture
of Calvary into the Missal,[1] both tended to make this formula
which opens with *Vere dignum* to be thought of as a preliminary,
a preface to the Eucharistic Prayer rather than its beginning,
and tended to obscure the fact that the prayer begins at the
previous *Dominus vobiscum*;[2] in fact this was forgotten, so that
we now get the inscription " Canon " (which means The
Formula—scil. of the Eucharistic Prayer) after the Preface.

After the series of thanksgivings the traditional form of the
Eucharistic Prayer went straight on to (**A**) the narrative of Our
Lord's institution of the Eucharist, beginning with a " who "
clause, as in our **Qui pridie quam pateretur** (" Who the
day before he suffered . . . "). Either the thanksgivings themselves mentioned Him prominently towards the end, or there
were a few words of transition mentioning Him, so that in either
case one went straight on with " Who the day before he suffered
. . . " to the account of the institution which includes the words
of consecration: " This is My Body . . . This is My Blood . . ."
The Prayer then continued with (**B**) some phrases expressing
the fact that " *we* " (this present group of the faithful) " *therefore* "
(i.e. because of Our Lord's institution just narrated and His
command to reiterate the offering) " *offer God this supreme Gift* ".
Then came (**C**) the conclusion in the form of a doxology (a declaring of God's glory[3]), to which the people all answered *Amen*.

Our present Eucharistic Prayer has all these elements. The

---

[1] See p. 110.

[2] The *Per omnia saecula saeculorum. Amen*, which are said aloud by the
priest and server just before this *Dominus vobiscum* belong, of course, to
the end of the Secret and not to the beginning of the Preface. They are
said aloud in order that the server may know when to answer *Amen*. It is
unfortunate that they give the impression of a beginning rather than an
ending—and this is still more unfortunate when the same thing happens
just before the *Pater Noster*: see p. 39.

[3] As in our " Glory be to the Father . . . "

priest concludes (**A**) the institution-narrative (i.e. the words of consecration) with Our Lord's command, **Haec quotiescumque . . . mei memoriam facietis** ("As often as you shall do these things you shall do them in memory of me "), which he takes up immediately after the elevation of the chalice with (**B**) the **Unde et memores . . . offerimus** ("Wherefore, O Lord, we . . . calling to mind . . . do offer") and two further prayers, the outline of which also goes back to the oldest records, expanding (**B**) the idea of our offering, the **Supra quae** ("Vouchsafe to look upon . . .") and the **Supplices** ("We most humbly beseech . . ."). The Latin words *memoriam* and *memores* show the connection of thought more clearly than do many English translations: " Our Lord said, ' Do this, calling Me to mind ', wherefore we, calling Him to mind . . . offer." This is the exact form which the Prayer takes in the very oldest text we know.

And finally in our Prayer comes (**C**) the great doxology, **Per ipsum et cum ipso** (" By/through Him and with Him . . . "), in which is expressed our certainty that by this offering to God of His own Son Incarnate we give supreme honour and glory to the Blessed Trinity. The **Amen** which all the people used to say here is really the great *Amen*, the central act of assent of the whole Mass, by which the people, even as they had affirmed their unity in the preceding Dialogue with what the priest was going to do, so now at the end of the Eucharistic Prayer affirm their full personal assent to all that he has done.[1] It is certainly a pity that, with the introduction of a silent Canon, the concluding *Per omnia saecula saeculorum*.[2] *Amen*, said aloud by priest and server, should sound more like the beginning of a new section of the Mass than the end of the Eucharistic Prayer.

The main outline of this Prayer, then, in our Missal is the same as that in the oldest Christian records of the third century; and we know that the general form of the Prayer goes

[1] If a homely translation may be permitted, *Amen* means " that goes for me too ".

[2] " . . . for ever and ever."

back to the Jewish thanksgiving-blessing which Our Lord used at the Last Supper for the framework of His own words of consecration and institution of the Sacrifice of the New Covenant. But our Canon has certain other formulas inserted into it, which are sometimes recognisable by the fact that they conclude with an *Amen* of their own.[1] This has the effect, when you *read* the Canon, of breaking up the unity of the Eucharistic Prayer by making it appear to be several prayers, each with its own conclusion; but as it is *said* this is not so: for the Preface begins aloud with the Dialogue and the Prayer ends aloud with *Per omnia saecula saeculorum. Amen*, the intervening *Amens* being said silently by the priest.

None of these inserted prayers is of very late growth, but they are additions to the Prayer as we know it in the earliest texts. It would therefore be wrong to give the impression that a fixed and traditional Eucharistic Prayer was somehow tampered with: rather, it is a question of the continual growth of the Prayer for the first six centuries, but always within a fixed form, from the earliest times when it was left to the apostle or bishop celebrating how exactly he would express the traditional thoughts of the Prayer to the time when the exact content and wording became fixed.

Earlier layer	
Preface	*Later layer*
	Te igitur
	Memento
	Communicantes
	Hanc igitur
(transition)	Quam oblationem
Qui pridie	
Unde et memores	
Supra quae	
Supplices	
	Memento etiam
	Nobis quoque
Per ipsum	
Amen.	

[1] So, the *Communicantes, Hanc igitur*, the *Memento* for the dead; and an *Amen* has been added to the *Supplices*.

The chief characteristic of these later insertions is that they are concerned with *naming* someone. First, in the **Te igitur** (" We therefore humbly pray . . . ") which now stands at the head of the Canon, we say *for whom* we want to offer this sacrifice—the whole Church of God, the Pope, our bishop, etc. At one time the (Christian) emperors got an honourable mention at this place. Then, in the **Memento for the Living** we continue this thought by naming, each one privately, our own friends and relatives, and ourselves (" and all here present ") —" for whom we offer this sacrifice of praise . . . " With the **Communicantes** (" Communicating with and honouring . . . ") begins the mention of those *with whom* we want to offer this sacrifice: here are named Our Lady, the apostles and—this being the rite which developed at Rome—some of the martyr Popes and other martyrs chiefly venerated at Rome. The leading idea is that of the *Communion* of Saints, the consciousness that the faithful living and dead form the one family of the Church, and that the Mass is the sacrifice of the Church. The next prayer, the **Hanc igitur** (" We therefore beseech thee . . . "), does not actually name anyone, but forms a sort of conclusion to this part of the Eucharistic Prayer, resuming in general terms all the intentions uppermost in our minds as we approach the actual climax of the Mass. The **Quam oblationem** (" Which oblation . . . ") serves as a link-prayer or transition to the institution-narrative itself, passing from the idea of our act of offering with which we have just been concerned (" Which offering . . . ") to the thought of what we are to offer, the Body and Blood of Our Lord, " Who the day before He suffered . . . "

The prayers inserted after the institution-narrative are again concerned with names. The **Memento etiam** (" Remember, O Lord, . . . "), which forms one prayer with **Ipsis, Domine** (" To these, O Lord, and to all who sleep in Christ . . . "), concluding with an *Amen*, is a Commemoration of the Dead and is followed by the **Nobis quoque peccatoribus** (" To us sinners also . . . ") which includes a second list of saints' names: John the Baptist, Stephen the first martyr, Matthias who took Judas' place, Barnabas the fellow-worker of St. Paul, and then more martyrs, men and women. At first sight this prayer naming the saints seems merely a repetition of the *Communicantes*, and there is no special reason why the dead should not be commemorated before the Consecration—they were sometimes; there is no essential difference between the thought of the " great dead ", the recognised saints of the Church, and our own personal dead. But between the two sets of prayers there is this difference: while the former looks ahead to the *sacrifice* about to be consummated, the prayers after the Consecration look ahead to the Eucharist as *sacrament*, to Holy Communion. There the thought was that we want to be united to the great saints of the Church in offering the sacrifice; here it is the hope that peace and rest may be granted to our dead and " to us sinners too ", so that we may all share together in the life of (commune with) the saints, by the power of the sacrament we are going to receive.

What has in fact happened in this development of the Canon is that *the ideas of the old Intercessory Prayers which occurred at the end of the Synaxis*,[1] though not their form, *have been trans-ferred to within the Eucharistic Prayer*. It would have been felt that the Eucharistic Prayer was *the* Prayer of the Church, and that any general prayers of the Church as a body—for her own welfare, for various classes of persons, and for all our intentions of any kind—rightly found their place within this Prayer.

The introduction of the names of the saints into the Canon is a result of the development in the fourth and fifth centuries of the Church's calendar and of the reverence paid to the martyrs and their places of burial. Our word " canonisation ",

[1] See pp. 27–28.

for the purpose of declaring some person worthy of public veneration as a saint, may be derived from the practice of including the names of such persons in the Canon of the Mass. Different churches would for a long time mention different names according as this or that saint was locally venerated. The list could not be extended indefinitely, and so some regulation was to be expected: the lists as we now have them in the *Communicantes* and *Nobis quoque peccatoribus* date from about the end of the sixth century.

The practice of **Elevation,** the raising up of the Host and then the chalice, after their consecration, for people to see, is not an early part of the Mass ritual, but, as now performed after the Consecration, only began in Europe in the eleventh century and did not become general till the thirteenth. Somewhat older is the so-called *Little Elevation* at the end of the Eucharistic Prayer, which goes back in Roman liturgy to the seventh century. At the words *omnis honor et gloria* (" . . . all honour and glory ") the priest raises Host and chalice together: this was never connected with the idea of the people seeing and venerating the consecrated elements, but is a gesture of offering. As we profess our faith at the end of the Eucharistic Prayer— and in that sense at its climax—that this offering to God is the greatest act of worship we could possibly perform or that He could receive, the priest accompanies this profession by his gesture of offering the Sacrament to God—the gifts of the faithful changed into the Body and Blood of Christ. The assent of the whole people is proclaimed by the great *Amen.*

THE BREAKING AND PATER NOSTER

Our Lord " blessed and *broke* and gave to His disciples ", and " The Breaking of Bread " was one of the earliest names for the Eucharist. As long as the bread consecrated at Mass was that provided by the faithful for the occasion, the actual breaking for distribution in Holy Communion was an essential and important part of the rite. It, or the ritual derived from it, is still important in the Eastern rites. We have quite detailed descriptions of how it was done in the Pope's Mass in the seventh century, but as it was performed silently, its falling out of the Mass, with the introduction of specially prepared small hosts, has not left much trace. Any necessary arrangement of the small hosts for Holy Communion was and is done during the Offertory.

What now occurs immediately after the Eucharistic Prayer is the saying of the **Pater Noster,** prefaced by a short introduction and extended by the *Libera* (" Deliver us, we beseech thee, O Lord . . . "). It was obviously fitting that Our Lord's own prayer should find a place in the Mass, and it is already firmly established in the Western rites by the fourth century. Its petition, " Give us this day our daily bread ", though primarily referring to all our needs, has obvious relevance to Holy Communion, so we might expect to find the *Pater* included in that part of the Mass which can be described as the Preparation for Communion. Gregory I placed it here so that it, and no merely man-made prayers, should come next after the Eucharistic Prayer. As this is a new and important moment in the Mass, it is prefaced by the invitation to prayer, *Oremus*, and an introduction, *Praeceptis salutaribus moniti* (" Instructed by Thy saving precepts . . . "), expressing our veneration for this prayer. The introduction, or some similar form of it, seems to have been there from the first inclusion of the *Pater* in the Mass.

The **Libera** takes up the last petition of the Our Father, *libera* (deliver) *nos a malo*, and forms a transition to the idea of peace, which is going to be prominent in the next stage of preparation for Holy Communion. The existence of such a prayer in all rites shows that it was a very early part of the Mass. While saying the conclusion of the *Libera* the priest **breaks** the Host in half, and then breaks a small piece off the left half, which piece, after *Pax Domini sit semper vobiscum* (" The peace of the Lord be always with you (plural) ") and the server's answer *Amen*, he places in the chalice, saying silently the **Haec commixtio** (" May this mingling . . . "). This ritual is a survival from at least one very ancient practice. In the fifth century (and a similar custom seems to go back to the second) the Pope or a bishop would break off portions of his consecrated Host at this place in the Mass and send them, by acolytes, to all the priests celebrating the Eucharist nearby, each of whom would place the piece so received in his own chalice at Mass:[1] this practice symbolised the real unity of the Eucharist as the one sacrifice of the Church and one with that of Calvary, in however many different places it might be celebrated; it was particularly appropriate coming at this point in the Mass when the prayers turn to the idea of peace—the concord and unity of the Church—before the reception of Communion. Another custom is less certain, that of preserving a piece of the consecrated Host (the *sancta*) from one Mass to the next Mass in the same church, during which it was placed in the chalice as a sign of the continuity and unity of the Eucharist in time: it seems at the most to have been a transitory custom round about the eighth century. Further, it was common to dip a piece of the Host in the unconsecrated wine given to the faithful after their Communion. Our present mingling of Bread and Wine, which is a mingling of the elements consecrated at the same Mass, serves to remind us of these old customs and to symbolise that the one Christ is fully present in both elements, so that the two together make one Sacrament. It had become a general practice by the eighth century, at which time, too, the accompanying prayer, *Haec commixtio*, originated.

[1] This piece came to be called the *fermentum* (leaven), the name being derived from Our Lord's parable of the leaven in Matt. xiii. 33.

THE COMMUNION

This covers all in our Mass from the *Agnus Dei* to the Post-Communion prayer. In the earliest days of the Church it was taken for granted that anyone who was rightfully present at all at the Eucharist received Holy Communion. " Partaking " in the Eucharist did not mean coming to say the customary prayers, still less just being there, but communicating. The Eucharist was the Supper of the Lord and one came to share in it. Those who had not been baptised, or Christians guilty of some grave sin who had not yet been reconciled to the Church, were simply excluded: they were ex-communicated. In the early Church it was quite a recognised practice for the faithful to take away with them the consecrated Bread after the Eucharist and keep It in their homes so that they could communicate on week-days, when the Eucharist was not usually celebrated. This may be regarded as a privilege arising in the days of persecution, when the faithful came to the Eucharist in peril of their lives, though it lasted for long after. Very similar practices have occurred in our own day in places like Dachau, in very similar circumstances.

The lamentable falling-off of the practice of frequent Communion, which began to some extent in Roman times and increased throughout the Middle Ages, is far too big a subject to be tackled here with any show of adequacy. Of the many contributory causes, ordinary human weakness and the fact that it was " easy " to be a Christian after the persecutions had ended in the fourth century seem to have been the least. More important were, first, the sudden influx into the Church of large numbers of barbarians accustomed to an exceedingly rough and ready mode of life, with the result that the authorities of the Church made stricter and stricter regulations; and, secondly, the long fight against Arianism, a heresy which denied the divinity of Christ: the Christian bishops were led to lay such emphasis on Our Lord's divinity in opposition to the heresy as to induce in the faithful a very deep-seated awe of the Blessed Sacrament and a fear of their own unworthiness. But the subject must be passed over here as being beyond our scope.

The celebrating bishop would first receive Holy Communion and then give It to the clergy present and the faithful; in the second century the deacons seem to have given It to the faithful, but their function soon came to be exclusively that of giving the chalice. As long as the custom of all present receiving Communion lasted, they received It in their places, the idea of their coming up to the altar beginning when only a few of those present communicated. At first, of course, Communion was always given under both kinds, but there were obvious reasons of hygiene, and the danger of spilling, which would cause the primitive practice to be at least modified. From the twelfth century the giving of the chalice to the faithful in any form dwindled rapidly in the West, but in the intervening centuries there had been intermediate practices, of giving the faithful a chalice of *unconsecrated* wine into which a few drops of the consecrated Wine had been poured, or into which a particle of the Host had been dipped—or simply unconsecrated wine, as is done today at the ordination of a priest after the bishop has given him Communion. The present-day practice in the Eastern rites, of dipping the Host in the consecrated chalice before placing It in the recipient's mouth, never seems to have been general in the West. All received the Bread in their hands right up to the ninth century, answering *Amen* to the priest's formula before receiving from the chalice, and this practice continued for some time longer in the case of the clergy.

The reception of Holy Communion was always primarily something done, and none of the forms of prayer connected with this part of the Mass is primitive. The oldest of them were (*a*) the Communion chant, (*b*) a formula used by the priest when giving Communion and (*c*) the Post-Communion prayer, a formal *oratio*: this shows a repetition of the pattern we have already met at the Introit and the Offertory—i.e. a movement of some sort, accompanied by a chant and concluded by a formal prayer.

But there was something done at the Communion which originated in the earliest times—the **Kiss of Peace,** which now only occurs at High Mass. In the earliest descriptions of the reception of catechumens into the Church on Easter morning we find that the new converts, after the initiation ceremonies of Baptism and Confirmation, were given the Kiss of Peace by the bishop and so led to their first Eucharist. The Kiss was their welcome into the Church, into communion with the faithful and so to a share, now their right, in the Supper of the Lord. From the very earliest times the Kiss of Peace appears as a feature of every Eucharist, symbolising the mutual love of the Christians of which the Eucharist was at once the greatest sign, the greatest cause and the greatest expression. At first, as still in the East, it seems to have come right at the beginning (when the Eucharist was held without the Synaxis) before the Offertory, because of Our Lord's injunction to " leave thy offering before the altar and go first to be reconciled to thy brother, and then coming thou shalt offer thy gift ".[1] But because of its connection with the unity of the Church and therefore with Holy Communion,[2] we find it coming just before Communion in Rome by the fourth century.

The **Pax Domini sit semper vobiscum** (" The peace of the Lord be always with you ") was originally the sign for the faithful to give each other the Kiss of Peace, but now it is said, just before the *Haec commixtio*, during the ritual of the mingling

---

[1] Matt. v. 23–24.
[2] The Eucharist is the *sacramentum unitatis ecclesiae* (sacrament of the unity of the Church)—i.e. the rite established by Our Lord to be a sign and an efficacious cause of unity.

of Bread and Wine. Both this and the threefold **Agnus Dei** therefore hover midway between Breaking and Communion: for the latter was first something like a chant to be sung during the Breaking, and only much later came to be regarded as part of the preparation for Communion, when the whole ritual of the Breaking had fallen into disuse. The cry *Agnus Dei* (" Lamb of God who takest away the sins of the world . . . "), like the *Kyrie*, is an acclamation to be sung by the people (both are now sung by the choir) and, again like the *Kyrie*, was imported into Rome from the East, only rather later and not till the seventh century. At first it would be repeated as often as necessary while the Breaking lasted, but the number settled down to three in about the ninth century.

As it now stands, with the third petition as *dona nobis pacem* (" Grant us peace "), this acclamation can rightly be thought of as part of the immediate preparation for Communion, which is dominated by the thought of peace and harmony in the Church, under the influence of the Kiss of Peace. We have already seen that the *Libera* passes from the last petition of the Our Father to the thought of peace;[1] then comes *Pax Domini sit semper vobiscum*, and then, after the *Haec commixtio*, the *Agnus Dei*. The next prayer, the first of three said silently by the priest as he bows over the centre of the altar, continues the idea of peace: this begins, **Domine Jesu Christe qui dixisti** (" O Lord Jesus Christ, who didst say to Thy apostles: Peace I leave you . . . "). It is in fact a prayer for the peace of the Church, and it is after it that the Kiss of Peace is given in High Mass. It is, however, of eleventh-century origin and began as a private devotion, as may be seen from the fact that it is addressed to Our Lord Himself[2] and mentions " *my* sins ".

We noted above that at first there was nothing *said* in connection with Communion, apart from the actual formula of

---

[1] *Da propitius pacem in diebus nostris*: " mercifully grant peace in our days."

[2] See p. 69.

distribution, and that the oldest prayers in this part of the Mass are the Communion chant, a formula for giving Holy Communion and the Post-Communion prayer. We now come to a number of prayers said in our present Mass which are all of comparatively late origin and all arose out of private devotion. They fall into two classes: those which arose out of the priest's private preparation and thanksgiving for Communion, and those which arose out of the people's preparation. The distinction must not be pressed too hard, because a number of these prayers were composed for the private use of either priest or people before they became a regular part of the Mass, and there is practically nothing in the Mass which the priest says just for himself and which does not " belong " equally to the people. But the wording of these prayers as they now stand owes more to their use by priests than by others. Their origin in private devotion shows why the " priest's " prayers are said silently.

Priest's Communion. We noted just above three prayers said silently by the priest as he bows over the altar after the *Agnus Dei,* of which the first is the prayer for peace. The other two, **Domine Jesu Christe, Fili Dei** (" O Lord Jesus Christ, Son of the living God . . . ") and **Perceptio** (" Let not the receiving of Thy Body . . . "), are both prayers for the priest's preparation for Communion, as may be seen from the fact that they are in the first person singular (" deliver me from all my iniquities . . . ", and " which I, all unworthy, presume to take ", etc.). Both declare their late and non-Roman origin by being addressed directly to Our Lord. They are first met with in " France " about the year A.D. 1000 as two among a variety of prayers from which the priest could choose. For a long time the prayers said still depended on choice or local usage, and these two were made fixed parts of the Mass only in the sixteenth century, by Pius V. The prayer **Panem coelestem** (" I will take the Bread of heaven . . . ") which the priest says next, while genuflecting, and one he says before consuming the chalice, **Quid retribuam** (" What return shall I make . . .?"), have an exactly similar history. We find among the various preparation prayers in use at this time certain sayings from the gospels, of which the words of the centurion to Our Lord, **Domine non sum dignus . . .** (" Lord, I am not worthy . . .")[1] are among the earliest used, but these too did not become fixed in the Roman Mass till Pius V. The reason why these first three words are said aloud, while all the rest of the prayers belonging to the priest's Communion are said inaudibly, is simply in order that the server may know when to ring the bell and so warn the people that Communion is being received; this practice may derive from a time when the priest would normally be the only person receiving, or the bell may have been a sign for the people to approach. To the same late period belongs the formula used immediately before the reception of the Host, **Corpus Domini nostri Jesu Christi,** and the parallel formula at the reception of the chalice, **Sanguis . . .** ("May the Body/Blood of Our Lord Jesus Christ . . ."). The priest also uses the first formula when giving Holy Communion, with the phrase "my soul" changed to "thy soul".

People's Communion. From the beginning *a* formula was used at the giving of Holy Communion, the oldest known in the Roman rite being "The bread of heaven in Christ Jesus", and another common one being simply "The Body of Christ" (*Corpus Christi*); in either case the recipient himself answered *Amen* as the Host was placed in his hands.

As has been said, the prayers in use for the priest's Communion were also for the use of the people. We find a more developed rite of giving Communion first appearing in the monasteries, and the *Confiteor, Misereatur* and *Indulgentiam* are transferred to the Mass from the Office in the thirteenth century, as during the opening prayers of Mass at the foot of

[1] Luke vii. 6; Matt. viii. 8.

the altar. We also find a dialogue occurring at this place, the priest asking the people for an act of faith in the Real Presence. But this had become by the sixteenth century a simple declaration by the priest, *Ecce Agnus Dei* ("Behold the Lamb of God. . . ."), which was often said in the vernacular up to the eighteenth century.

The **Communion Chant,** meant to be sung during the distribution of Communion, seems to be the oldest of the three chants by the choir; all came in at about the same time, viz. fourth-fifth centuries. Like the other two, Introit and Offertory chant, it was at first a full psalm, but shrank in the course of time as the practice of all receiving Communion dwindled, until we now have only the antiphon left. As it was intended to accompany the Communion of the people, it was begun after the priest's Communion, so that, when it became common for there to be no other Communions but the priest's, the idea became fixed that it belonged after the Communion, for which it came to be thought of as a thanksgiving. The result is that now the choir at High Mass sing it during the Ablutions, even when there are other Communions, and the priest reads it when he has finished the Ablutions.

After his own Communion and that of the faithful the priest performs the Ablutions: that is, he collects with the paten any particles of the Host that may be lying on the corporal[1], and places them in the chalice, into which the server pours first wine and then both wine and water (over the priest's fingers into the chalice), which the priest then drinks. Thus all that has come into contact with the sacred elements is cleansed. While doing this he says two prayers, **Quod ore sumpsimus** ("Grant, Lord, that what we have taken . . .") and **Corpus tuum Domine,** ("May Thy Body, O Lord, which I have received, . . .") which are both of medieval

[1] The paten is a concave metal plate, gold or gilded; for further details of its use see p. 155. The corporal is a square of linen in the centre of the altar on which both Host and chalice are placed.

origin, like all the prayers at this part of the Mass, and have the character of a thanksgiving for Communion.

The **Post-Communion** is the third of the *orationes* or formal prayers said by the priest in the name of the whole people; it concludes the Communion rite by a sort of summing-up, as the Collect concludes the Entrance rite and the Secret the Offertory. Like the other two *orationes* it varies with the feast or occasion and is prefaced by *Dominus vobiscum. Et cum spiritu tuo. Oremus.* The earliest records in other rites of a prayer in this place show that its character was that of a thanksgiving for Communion. But Roman liturgy, introducing this prayer in the fifth century, modelled it on the other *orationes* as a petition, usually for the full fruits and graces of Communion—a petition addressed to God "through Christ Our Lord". The thanksgiving character is preserved indirectly by the reference to the Gift received.

CONCLUSION

We would naturally expect there to be some sort of formal conclusion to the Eucharist, and this from the earliest times was a form of Dismissal spoken by the deacon. Our present dismissal, **Ite Missa est**[1], still chanted by the deacon at High Mass, is prefaced by *Dominus vobiscum* which we have often met elsewhere as a greeting to capture the attention of the congregation. It goes back to the 4th century when the word *Missa* had come to have its technical sense.[2] The answer, *Deo gratias*, ("Thanks be to God") was returned by the people as a final act of thanksgiving. Our present practice of substituting for this dismissal *Benedicamus Domino* ("Let us bless the Lord") on days when there is no *Gloria*, and *Requiescant in pace* ("May they rest in peace") at Masses for the dead, is of late medieval

[1] Usually translated, " Go, the Mass is ended "; but literally, " Go, this is the Dismissal."

[2] See p. 181.

origin. Of similar date too is the prayer **Placeat** ("Let the performance of my homage . . .") which the priest next says bowing over the centre of the altar, as may be seen from the fact that it is in the singular ("the sacrifice which I, though unworthily, have offered") and said silently. All have, of course, offered the sacrifice, but the priest's function of offering is special to himself and different from everyone else's. He alone has stood at the altar and this is his private prayer, before he leaves it, that God may be pleased with his sacrifice. The kiss of the altar balances the kiss on arrival and the *Placeat* balances the prayer *Oramus te Domine* there said,[1] also in a bowing posture.

From very early times we find the conclusion of the Mass connected with some kind of **Blessing,** though it took many different forms in different times and places. For long it was a blessing given by the Pope or bishop to his ministers and the people on his way out after the *Ite Missa est*, and so was not really a part of the Mass, which ended with the dismissal. Nor did priests give this blessing at first, though they seem to have done so quite commonly by the seventh century, at least outside Rome. By the twelfth century we find the blessing being given by the celebrant from the altar before going out, and the Sign of the Cross and accompanying formula, *Benedicat vos omnipotens Deus* ("May God almighty bless you (plural) . . ."), come from the same time. Before that there had been various similar formulas, and the act of blessing consisted in the words and not in a gesture. The omission of the blessing at Masses for the dead is a sixteenth century innovation.

The reading of the **Last Gospel,** the first fourteen verses of St. John's gospel, is one of the latest additions to the Mass. A special devotion to this Prologue of St. John, which asserts the divinity of Christ so clearly, had arisen in France as a result of the long struggle against Arianism,[2] but we first hear of its

[1] See p. 62.   [2] See p. 46.

being read at the end of the Mass there in the twelfth century. It was still not a general practice in the Roman rite in the sixteenth century, and where it did occur was often said by the priest walking away from the altar, as a bishop still says it. Mass had traditionally ended with a cry of thanksgiving by the people, so now too the server says at the end of the Last Gospel—*Deo gratias!*

CHAPTER V

The Prayers of the Mass

ENTRANCE RITE

At the foot of the altar

Sacerdos. In nomine Patris, et Filii, et Spiritus Sancti. Amen.

Introibo ad altare Dei.
Minister. Ad Deum qui laetificat juventutem meam.
S. Judica me Deus et discerne causam meam de gente non sancta: ab homine iniquo et doloso erue me.

M. Quia tu es Deus fortitudo mea: quare me reppulisti, et quare tristis incedo, dum affligit me inimicus?
S. Emitte lucem tuam, et veritatem tuam: ipsa me deduxerunt, et adduxerunt in montem sanctum tuum, et in tabernacula tua.
M. Et introibo ad altare Dei: ad Deum qui laetificat juventutem meam.
S. Confitebor tibi in cithara, Deus, Deus meus: quare tristis es anima mea, et quare conturbas me?

M. Spera in Deo, quoniam adhuc confitebor illi: salutare vultus mei, et Deus meus.
S. Gloria Patri, et Filio, et Spiritui Sancto.
M. Sicut erat in principio, et nunc, et semper: et in saecula saeculorum. Amen.
S. Introibo ad altare Dei.
M. Ad Deum qui laetificat juventutem meam.

Priest. In the name of the Father, and of the Son, and of the Holy Ghost. Amen.
I will go unto the altar of God.
Server. To God, who giveth joy to my youth.
P. Judge me, O God, and distinguish my cause from the nation that is not holy; from the unjust and deceitful man deliver me.
S. For Thou, O God, art my strength: why hast Thou cast me off? And why go I sorrowful, whilst the enemy afflicteth me?
P. Send forth Thy light and Thy truth: they have led me, and brought me unto Thy holy hill, and into Thy tabernacles.
S. And I will go unto the altar of God; unto God who giveth joy to my youth.
P. Upon the harp I will praise Thee, O God my God: why art Thou sad, O my soul, and why dost thou disquiet me?
S. Hope in God, for I shall yet praise Him, who is the salvation of my countenance, and my God.
P. Glory be to the Father, and to the Son, and to the Holy Ghost.
S. As it was in the beginning, is now, and ever shall be, world without end. Amen.
P. I will go unto the altar of God.
S. Unto God, who giveth joy to my youth.

In nomine Patris . . .

Misereatur tui . . .

In nomine Patris. This is the formal beginning of the Prayers of Preparation, which, as we have seen, differed widely in the Middle Ages during the years of their formation. The Sign of the Cross would be made wherever these prayers were understood to begin—sometimes before vesting, sometimes after putting on the chasuble and before setting out for the altar, eventually at the altar's foot. When these prayers began in the sacristy the Introit was the real beginning of Mass, and we still have a Sign of the Cross accompanying its opening words.

Judica. ("Judge me, O God, . . .") The psalm is said in full with its antiphon before and after, as in the Office; the antiphon verse, *Introibo ad altare Dei* . . . ("I will go unto the altar of God . . ."), is the "operative" verse, the one for which the psalm was chosen as being appropriate to this occasion.

The antiphon was a musical necessity, a verse of a psalm sung first by the cantor to show what tune was going to be used before the psalm itself was started (the use of musical instruments for long being regarded as "pagan"); two halves of the choir would then, in the Office, sing the psalm answering each other verse by verse. There is, however, an older type of psalmody which we meet in liturgy, Responsory singing: here a verse or versicle (part of a verse) was sung by the cantor, repeated by everyone, and again repeated by them after every verse of the psalm. This goes right back to Jewish practice, and belongs to congregational singing before there was any semi-professional body to take over (and perhaps monopolise) the chant[1]. There would not be "books" to go round, and anyway people could not read; so by this method the whole congregation could join in a psalm, while only the cantor needed a book. Some of the psalms were written to be sung this way, e.g. Ps. cxxxv. which repeats "for his mercy endureth

[1] The *Invitatorium* at Matins preserves an example of responsory singing.

for ever" after every new phrase. It is possibly in imitation of this type of singing that we find in antiphonal singing the antiphon repeated at the end of the psalm: it gave the congregation a chance to join in.

S. Adjutorium nostrum in nomine Domini.

M. Qui fecit coelum et terram.

S. Confiteor Deo omnipotenti, etc.

M. Misereatur tui omnipotens Deus, et dimissis peccatis tuis, perducat te ad vitam aeternam.

S. Amen.

M. Confiteor Deo omnipotenti, beatae Mariae semper Virgini, beato Michaeli Archangelo, beato Joanni Baptistae, sanctis Apostolis Petro et Paulo, omnibus sanctis, et tibi pater: quia peccavi nimis cogitatione, verbo, et opere: mea culpa, mea culpa, mea maxima culpa. Ideo precor beatam Mariam semper Virginem, beatum Michaelem Archangelum, beatum Joannem Baptistam, sanctos Apostolos Petrum et Paulum, omnes sanctos, et te, pater, orare pro me ad Dominum Deum nostrum.

S. Misereatur vestri omnipotens Deus, et dimissis peccatis vestris, perducat vos ad vitam aeternam.

M. Amen.

S. Indulgentiam, absolutionem et remissionem peccatorum nostrorum, tribuat nobis omnipotens et misericors Dominus.

M. Amen.

S. Deus tu conversus vivificabis nos.

M. Et plebs tua laetabitur in te.

S. Ostende nobis, Domine, misericordiam tuam.

M. Et salutare tuum da nobis.

S. Domine exaudi orationem meam.

M. Et clamor meus ad te veniat.

S. Dominus vobiscum.

M. Et cum spiritu tuo.

S. Oremus.

P. Our help is in the name of the Lord.

S. Who made heaven and earth.

P. I confess to almighty God, etc.

S. May almighty God be merciful to thee, and forgiving thy sins bring thee to everlasting life.

P. Amen.

S. I confess to almighty God, to blessed Mary ever a Virgin, to blessed Michael the Archangel, to blessed John the Baptist, to the holy Apostles Peter and Paul, to all the saints, and to you, Father, that I have sinned exceedingly, in thought, word and deed, through my fault, through my fault, through my most grievous fault. Therefore, I beseech blessed Mary ever a Virgin, blessed Michael the Archangel, blessed John the Baptist, the holy Apostles Peter and Paul, and all the saints, and you, Father, to pray to the Lord our God for me.

P. May almighty God be merciful unto you, and forgiving you your sins bring you to life everlasting.

S. Amen.

P. May the almighty and merciful Lord grant us pardon, absolution and remission of our sins.

S. Amen.

P. Thou shalt turn again, O God, and wilt quicken us.

S. And Thy people will rejoice in Thee.

P. Show us, O Lord, Thy mercy.

S. And grant us Thy salvation.

P. O Lord, hear my prayer.

S. And let my cry come unto Thee.

P. The Lord be with you.

S. And with thy spirit.

P. Let us pray.

Aufer a nobis, quaesumus Domine, iniquitates nostras: ut ad Sancta sanctorum puris mereamur mentibus introire. Per Christum Dominum nostrum. Amen.	Take away from us our iniquities, we beseech Thee, O Lord, that we may be worthy to enter with pure minds into the Holy of Holies. Through Christ our Lord. Amen.
Oramus te, Domine, per merita sanctorum tuorum, quorum reliquiae hic sunt, et omnium sanctorum: ut indulgere digneris omnia peccata mea. Amen.	We beseech Thee, O Lord, by the merits of Thy saints whose relics are here, and of all the saints, that Thou wouldst vouchsafe to forgive all my sins. Amen.

Confiteor, etc. ("I confess . . ." etc.) The form of Confession of sinfulness, preceded by *Adiutorium* ("Our help is in the name of the Lord") and followed by the Absolution, is found here just as it occurs in the Office (Prime and Compline), whence it was borrowed to form part of the Prayers of Preparation about A.D. 1000. It takes the place of the silent prayer which the celebrant made prostrate before the altar at least as early as the seventh century. The actual *Confiteor* we now use developed from the twelfth to the fourteenth centuries. The Absolution consists of two prayers invoking God's forgiveness, *Misereatur* ("May almighty God . . .") and *Indulgentiam* ("May the almighty and merciful Lord . . ."), which are also used by the priest in Confession just before he pronounces the actual forgiveness.[1] In both Office and Mass there follows a dialogue of versicles from the psalms, *Deus tu conversus*, etc. ("Thou shalt turn again, O God, . . .").

Aufer and **Oramus.** Finally there is a *Dominus vobiscum*, followed by a formal prayer, *Aufer* (" Take away from us our iniquities . . . "), which the priest says as he goes up the steps to the altar. Before becoming part of the Mass the Prayers of Preparation had, in the monasteries, grown almost into part of the Office, a " Little Hour " on their own, so they are made to conclude like such Hours with a Collect preceded by *Dominus vobiscum*, which has here lost its character as a

---

[1] These prayers were regarded as a form of general absolution at least until the scholastic theologians had developed the doctrine of the sacraments.

greeting and is not said facing the congregation. The previous prayers are said aloud because they have to be answered, but *Aufer* and *Oramus te Domine* ("We beseech thee, O Lord, . . .") are said silently. *Aufer* is an old Roman *oratio*, though its insertion here is late, but *Oramus* is a later composition (it is in the singular at the end, the priest directing our prayers to his sins); the priest begins it bowing over the altar and kisses the altar in the middle of it: this is known to be an old pagan practice, one of the many such practices baptised by the Christians—i.e. given a Christian use and meaning. The kiss of the altar in veneration for its sanctity, both as the altar of sacrifice and the common table of the household of God, is early, but the insertion of a prayer during the action is medieval.

This prayer, the *Oramus*, refers to the relics of the saint(s) which are now set into every altar-stone, and the altar is kissed at their mention. The celebration of Mass in a cemetery church built over the grave of a martyr is very early, but the association of the altar itself with relics is a later idea, which various causes helped to develop. It was never obligatory in the Middle Ages to insert relics into an altar-stone, but it was quite common by the eleventh century. The meaning of the kiss, therefore, is primarily veneration for the altar itself, and its extension to all other places in the Mass from this one followed in the eleventh and twelfth centuries. The priest now kisses the altar before turning his back on it, except when the Blessed Sacrament is on it, when he genuflects.

SINGING IN THE MASS. The Introit, Offertory and Communion chants, each covering some sort of protracted action or procession, always seem to have belonged to some kind of professional choir, the *schola cantorum*.

Of the remaining sung parts of the Mass (apart from anything intoned by the celebrant alone), what one would like to be able

Oramus te Domine . . . quorum reliquiae hic sunt

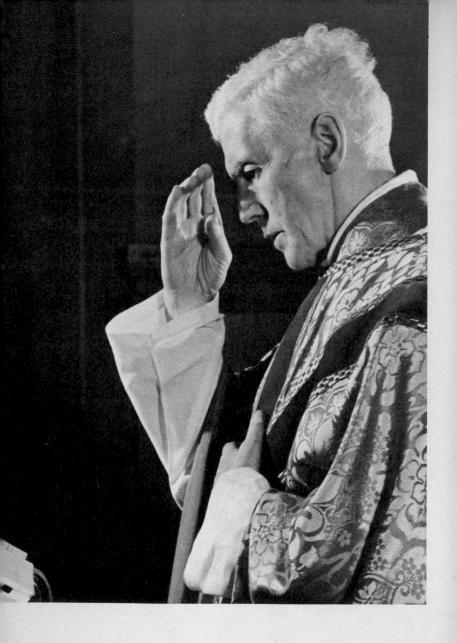

Introit

to say is that they were really meant for the whole body of the faithful to sing together or to take their part in. And not only does it seem natural for the people to sing, and very likely that they would have done, but the *Kyrie, Gloria, Sanctus* and *Agnus Dei* all have their origins in popular hymns and acclamations, while the *Gradual*, both in its Jewish ancestry and its construction, points to a type of singing specifically arranged so that the people could take their part in it, even if unfamiliar with the language.

Still, however much truth there may be in these remarks, it would be wrong to give the impression that one can put one's finger on a particular date and say that *then* the people used to join in all these chants. Particularly at Rome. For it seems that the revision made by Gregory I was a chastening and simplifying of a chant which had already grown florid, and therefore beyond the capacity of a congregation, *before* the introduction of *Kyrie, Gloria* or *Agnus Dei* into the Roman Mass.

The evidence is scanty and debatable, and mainly concerned with big churches and big functions. One suspects that a lot more popular singing took place in smaller churches than such evidence would lead one to suppose.

INTROIT

[*By way of illustration, the Proper of the first (Midnight) Mass for Christmas Day will be given throughout, except for the Preface*]

(Ps. ii. 7): Dominus dixit ad me: Filius meus es tu, ego hodie genui te.

The Lord hath said to Me: Thou art My Son, this day have I begotten Thee.

(Ps. ii. 1): Quare fremuerunt gentes: et populi meditati sunt inania?

Why have the gentiles raged, and the people devised vain things?

Gloria Patri, et Filio, et Spiritui Sancto.

Glory be to the Father, and to the Son, and to the Holy Ghost.

Sicut erat in principio, et nunc, et semper, et in saecula saeculorum. Amen.

As it was in the beginning, is now, and ever shall be, world without end. Amen.

Dominus dixit ad me: Filius meus es tu, ego hodie genui te.

The Lord hath said to Me: Thou art My Son, this day have I begotten Thee.

S. Kyrie eleison.	Lord, have mercy.
M. Kyrie eleison.	Lord, have mercy.
S. Kyrie eleison.	Lord, have mercy.
M. Christe eleison.	Christ, have mercy.
S. Christe eleison.	Christ, have mercy.
M. Christe eleison.	Christ, have mercy.
S. Kyrie eleison.	Lord, have mercy.
M. Kyrie eleison.	Lord, have mercy.
S. Kyrie eleison.	Lord, have mercy.

Introit. What remains now of the Introit is the antiphon, one verse of the psalm (usually either the first verse or that following the antiphon verse), the concluding *Gloria Patri* and the antiphon repeated. The psalm was chosen, when some special occasion was being celebrated, for an appropriate idea that occurred in one of the verses, but often this verse has disappeared in the process of abbreviation.' For example, our third Mass on Christmas Day has in the Introit the first verse of Ps. xcvii, " Sing ye to the Lord a new canticle, because he hath done wonderful things "; but the psalm was chosen for this Mass for its second verse, " The Lord hath made known His salvation, He hath revealed His justice in the sight of the gentiles ", which now no longer appears. The same process of truncation often explains the apparent irrelevance of many of the chants in our missal—Gradual, Offertory and Communion chants, as well as Introit. The concluding of all psalms with the *Gloria Patri* originated in Antioch in the fourth century as a protest against Arianism; the second half, *Sicut erat* ("As it was in the beginning . . . "), was a Western addition of the sixth century, directed against those heretics who denied the eternity of the Son. The custom of the priest reading this and the other chants from the missal must have come pretty early in private Masses, though it is first attested in the seventh century. As late as the thirteenth century they were not always read by the priest at a Mass at which they were being sung. Some of the Introits, composed after it had been cut down, have an antiphon from a different psalm than the verse or from a different part of the Bible than the psalms. The Introits, Offertory and Communion chants of the Sundays after Pentecost show a progress through the Book of Psalms, a verse being taken here and there, as there is no particular theme which suggests itself as appropriate during this time.

Kyrie. This acclamation is also a pagan practice baptised by the Christians, which belonged in paganism to sun-worship among other cults. The idea of Our Lord as *Sol Oriens*, the Rising Sun, who came up on Easter Sunday from the darkness of the grave, the light of the world (John i. 5, ix. 5, xii. 46, etc.), quite captivated the minds of the early Christians, and shows itself in many ways—e.g. in their facing towards the East to greet the Risen Christ, just as pagans turned themselves towards the rising sun to pray. The worship of *Sol Invictus* (The Unconquered Sun) was introduced into pagan Rome in 275, as an attempt to lead the Romans towards some form of monotheism; the feast was December 25th. By the beginning of the fourth century we first find Christmas being celebrated on that day. It is now almost certain that December 25th was chosen for Christmas Day to " baptise " the pagan practice and to provide a Christian counter-feast.

Kyrie (" Lord "), therefore, is addressed to Our Lord: *Christe eleison* is a Roman invention. The regulation of the acclamation to three sets of three inevitably caused people to think of the Blessed Trinity—*Kyrie* for the Father, *Christe* for the Son, *Kyrie* again for the Holy Spirit—but this is a later idea and the whole acclamation is really addressed to Christ. In general, it is against the whole trend and spirit of the Roman liturgy (at any rate for the priest) to direct prayers immediately *to* Christ, and this first came in with these popular acclamations, the *Kyrie* and the *Agnus Dei*. In Rome about 600 the *Kyrie* was sung alternately by clergy and people, and this seems a fairly clear case of the increasing intricacy of the music causing the chant to be relegated eventually to the choir; where a simple tone is used for it and all the congregation join in, we are nearest to its traditional use and meaning.

Gloria in excelsis Deo. Et in terra pax hominibus bonae voluntatis. Laudamus te. Benedicimus te. Adoramus te. Glorificamus te. Gratias agimus tibi propter magnam gloriam tuam. Domine Deus, Rex coelestis, Deus Pater omnipotens. Domine Fili unigenite, Jesu Christe. Domine Deus, Agnus Dei, Filius Patris. Qui tollis peccata mundi, miserere nobis. Qui tollis peccata mundi, suscipe deprecationem nostram. Qui sedes ad dexteram Patris, miserere nobis. Quoniam tu solus sanctus. Tu solus Dominus. Tu solus altissimus, Jesu Christe, cum sancto Spiritu, in gloria Dei Patris. Amen.

Glory be to God on high, and on earth peace to men of good will. We praise Thee, we bless Thee, we adore Thee, we glorify Thee. We give Thee thanks for Thy great glory, O Lord God, heavenly King, God the Father Almighty. O Lord Jesus Christ, the only begotten Son; O Lord God, Lamb of God, Son of the Father, who takest away the sins of the world, have mercy on us. Who takest away the sins of the world, receive our prayers. Who sittest at the right hand of the Father, have mercy on us. For Thou only art holy, Thou only art the Lord, Thou only, O Jesus Christ, together with the Holy Ghost, art most high in the glory of God the Father. Amen.

Gloria. (" Glory to God in the highest . . . "). The early Church was very rich in hymns, but they came to be replaced by the use of psalms because of the feeling that " God's word " was better than anything composed by man. This hymn is a particularly elaborate form of doxology, or acclamation of the Trinity, of which many examples are found already in the Epistles of the New Testament, particularly in their opening and closing phrases; see the long ones in Eph. i. 2–14, 1 Pet. i. 3–12; and shorter ones in 2 Pet. iii. 18, Jude 25. Other examples we have seen in the short *Gloria Patri* just mentioned and in the *Per ipsum* etc., which concludes the Eucharistic Prayer. As may be seen clearly from this latter example, with its *est tibi . . . gloria* (" is to thee all . . . glory "), all these doxologies are really statements of fact and not wishes; so the Anglican conclusion of the Our Father, " for thine is the kingdom . . . ", is a more correct doxology than our own translation, " Glory *be* to the Father . . . " and " Glory *be* to God

Kyrie eleison

Gloria in excelsis Deo

in the highest . . . " The *Gloria* has many similar forms in both East and West, and is quoted by St. Athanasius in the middle of the fourth century as the Morning Hymn; parts of it are attested in the second century. It was not used in the Mass at Rome till the early sixth century and then only at the bishop's Mass, and in a priest's Mass only at Easter: in either case it was sung by the whole people. Its length saved the chant from becoming too intricate and fortunately it is often still sung by the congregation, at least alternately with the choir.

COLLECT(S)

S. Dominus vobiscum.
M. Et cum spiritu tuo.
S. Oremus.

P. The Lord be with you.
S. And with thy spirit.
P. Let us pray.

Deus, qui hanc sacratissimam noctem veri luminis fecisti illustratione clarescere: da, quaesumus; ut, cuius lucis mysteria in terra cognovimus, eius quoque gaudiis in coelo perfruamur: Qui tecum. . . .

O God, who hast made this most sacred night to shine forth with the brightness of the true light, grant, we beseech Thee, that we may enjoy His happiness in heaven, the mystery of whose light we have known upon earth: who liveth and reigneth with Thee, in the unity of the Holy Spirit, God for ever and ever.

M. Amen.

S. Amen.

Collect. This formal *oratio* as it now stands in the Mass is the conclusion of the Entrance Rite. It occurs also in the Intercessory Prayers; this and the fact that the Greek form of intercession is a litany of petitions, each answered by the people with *Kyrie eleison,* suggest that *Kyrie* and Collect belong together, the latter summing up and concluding the litany which, with the *Gloria,* was the people's part in the rite of Entrance. The name " Collect " is connected both with the " gathering " place, the church (the Mass itself was sometimes called *collecta* in persecution times), and with the idea of "gathering together" and resuming the people's litany in a formal and concluding prayer.

The *Dominus vobiscum* here has the full force of a greeting,[1] and both Synaxis and Eucharist seem to have begun and ended with a greeting. *Pax vobis*, which was Our Lord's greeting at Easter to His apostles, came to be reserved for bishops who still use it at this point. The *Oremus* is the shortest form of invitation to prayer; the longer one included *Flectamus genua* and *Levate*, with a pause between them while everyone was down on both knees: a trace of this is left in the bow which the priest makes at the word *Oremus*.

The priest's posture at this and other formal prayers and during most of the Eucharistic Prayer—he stands with hands opened in front of him—was a pagan attitude taken up before the rising sun, which the Christians adopted and baptised. Well into the Middle Ages the people too stood in this posture when the priest did. During the prayers which arose from private devotion the usual posture is that of joined hands, which is of German medieval origin.

The early Roman Collects (and other *orationes*), formed between the third and sixth centuries, have a characteristic brevity and clarity; see, for example, those of the Sundays after Pentecost. The usual pattern is: " O God, who . . .: grant, we beseech Thee; . . . through Jesus Christ . . . " The who-clause was made an occasion for bringing in a reference to the saint of the day in a saint's Mass. Well into the Middle Ages the general rule persisted that the Mass and the priest's prayers in it are directed to God the Father, through Christ Our Lord, who is not addressed immediately. The lengthy Collects and those addressed to Christ are of late origin.[2] And for long too the Roman rule was for no more than one *oratio* to be said in a Mass, the practice of commemorating concurrent feasts being medieval.

---

[1] Our salutation " Good-bye " = God-be-with-ye = *Dominus vobiscum*.
[2] An apparent exception are the Collects for the Sundays of Advent, but these seem to have been changed, and it is not clear when this took place.

Dominus vobiscum

Oremus before the Collect

SYNAXIS

EPISTLE

Lectio Epistolae beati Pauli Apostoli ad Titum.	The Lesson from the Epistle of the blessed Apostle Paul to Titus.

Dearly beloved: The grace of God our Saviour hath appeared to all men. . . . These things speak and exhort, in Christ Jesus Our Lord (*Tit. ii.* 11–15).

M. Deo gratias.	*S.* Thanks be to God.

Epistle. When the Roman rite cut its lessons down from three to two, except on Ember days and a few others, a lesson from the Old Testament was usually kept for ferial Masses (e.g. the weekdays in Lent), the passages being chosen for their prophetic value. Sometimes the passage has a connection with the stational church in which the Pope was going to say Mass (cf. Appendix I). There seems to have been as early as the fifth century a regular plan for Epistles and Gospels to cover as much of the New Testament as possible, but the multiplication of feast days, as the Church's calendar grew, and the choice of appropriate passages for their Masses, soon put an end to any very orderly scheme.

From the earliest times we hear of some sort of raised lectern being in use for the Lessons, with the reader facing the congregation. (It must be borne in mind that in a solemn Mass the celebrant for long had nothing to do with the Epistle or Gospel, any more than with the chants.) The Jews had used such a lectern in their synagogues. In Christian churches the lectern soon developed into the raised Ambo or pulpit, with steps leading up to it, very much the same as our own; and from this the chants too were sung before the full development of choirs. The choice of its situation in the church seems to have been for long directed by suitability for the purpose of being heard. Our present practice of reading the Gospel on the north side of a church (which faces east), with the deacon facing north in High Mass, and the Epistle on the south side, does not appear till the tenth century. Contemporary reasons given for the custom are rather queer—such as, that the north was the region of the heathen or of the devil, who needed the Gospel most! The real origin of the practice is rather obscure: more likely explanations are that the women occupied the north side of the church, and it was more fitting for the deacon, when the lessons were read facing the congregation, to read from the north side facing across to the men; or, more simply, that priests saying private Masses had come to read the Gospel at the north side of the altar, because the other side needed to be kept clear for the Offertory preparations; or, that at a bishop's Mass the reader would want to take up a position where he was facing both the bishop's *cathedra* and the people.

GRADUAL, ALLELUIA (TRACT, SEQUENCE)

(Ps. cix. 3, 1): Tecum principium in die virtutis tuae: in splendoribus sanctorum, ex utero ante luciferum genui te.

Dixit Dominus Domino meo: Sede a dextris meis: donec ponam inimicos tuos, scabellum pedum tuorum.

Alleluia, alleluia.

(Ps. ii. 7): Dominus dixit ad me: Filius meus es tu, ego hodie genui te.

Alleluia.

With thee is the principality in the day of thy strength: in the brightness of the saints, from the womb before the day-star I begot thee.

The Lord said to my Lord: Sit Thou at My right hand: until I make Thy enemies Thy footstool.

Alleluia, alleluia.

The Lord hath said to Me: Thou art My Son, this day have I begotten Thee.

Alleluia.

The book being now removed to the Gospel side, the Priest stands at the middle of the altar, and says

Munda cor meum, ac labia mea, omnipotens Deus, qui labia Isaiae prophetae calculo mundasti ignito: ita me tua grata miseratione dignare mundare, ut sanctum Evangelium tuum digne valeam nuntiare. Per Christum Dominum nostrum. Amen.

Cleanse my heart and my lips, O almighty God, who didst cleanse the lips of the prophet Isaias with a burning coal; and vouchsafe, through Thy gracious mercy, so to purify me, that I may worthily proclaim Thy holy Gospel. Through Christ our Lord. Amen.

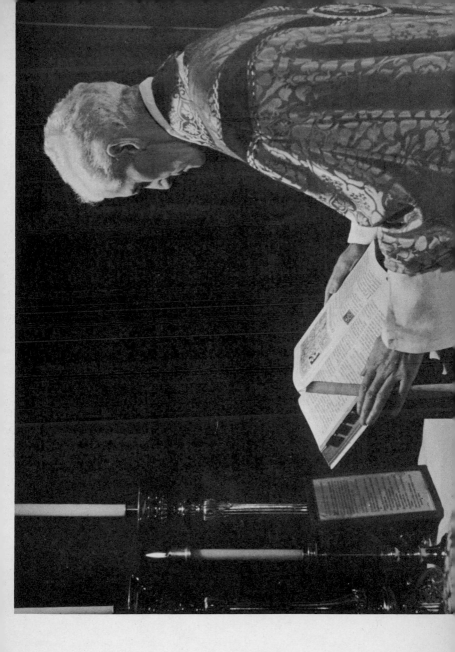

Epistle

Gradual, etc.

Jube, Domine, benedicere.	Lord, give Thy blessing.
Dominus sit in corde meo, et in labiis meis: ut digne et competenter annuntiem Evangelium suum. Amen.	May the Lord be in my heart and on my lips, that I may worthily and in a becoming manner announce His holy Gospel. Amen.

Gradual. Alleluia. Tract. Sequence. The psalmody at this point is the oldest singing of the Christian liturgy, derived from synagogue practice,[1] and the old type of Responsory singing which prevailed till the fourth century was used for it[2]— not the antiphonal singing by two half-choirs, as was customary in the later chants (Introit, Offertory, Communion). Only one singer with a " book " was needed here; he sang from the Ambo facing the people, who replied to him with the same versicle, chosen from the psalm in question, all through. The Gradual (*gradus*, a step) is so called because sung from the steps of the Ambo. It seems to have been the psalmody which took place after the Old Testament lection when there were still three, the Alleluia being the one which came in between Epistle and Gospel, the second and third lections. Now that there are only two, we get Gradual and Alleluia following each other after the Epistle. All that is left of the Gradual is the responsory versicle and one verse of the psalm—often the next verse after the versicle.

The Alleluia follows the same pattern of responsory singing, those psalms being chosen which were written to have the cry *Alleluia* (" praise God ") repeated after every verse. The versicle *Alleluia* was sung first by the cantor, repeated by all, and then repeated again after every verse; hence we get the pattern of our psalmody, *Alleluia, Alleluia* . . . (psalm verse) . . . *Alleluia*. When there is a Sequence the last *Alleluia* comes after it. In Paschal time the Gradual, which—like the Old Testament lection—has affinities with penitential seasons, is dropped and we get a double Alleluia instead, i.e. a second psalm verse again followed by *Alleluia*; the Gradual, however,

[1] See pp. 25–6.   [2] See p. 59.

is not dropped during Easter week itself as the psalm used throughout is Ps. cxvii, which is specially the Easter psalm.

The Tract is substituted for the Alleluia on more penitential occasions, as during Lent; it is like the Gradual in form, only with more verses. The name may be from the chant used, or the versicle may never have been repeated after each verse and the chant therefore called the " drawn out " chant.

Sequences developed in the early Middle Ages as flourishes and variations of the Alleluia melody.[1] Our present type of Sequence, an independent hymn, came later and a great crop of them appeared in Gallican lands; but Rome was always very chary of them, and Pius V kept only four—*Victimae Paschali* (Easter), *Veni Sancte Spiritus* (Pentecost) an eleventh-century hymn, *Lauda Sion*[2] (Corpus Christi), and the *Dies Irae*; the *Stabat Mater*, composed in the fourteenth century, was transferred from the Office to the Missal in the seventeenth.

Munda cor meum, etc. As early as the seventh century we find the deacon, before going in procession to read the gospel, asking the celebrant on his knees for a blessing, which was given with the words *Dominus sit in corde tuo* . . . , or some similar formula. The form of asking, *Iube domne benedicere* (" Lord, give Thy blessing "), is a bit later.[3] The prefacing of this request by the prayer *Munda cor meum*, with its reference to Isa. vi. 6–7, said by the priest bowing over the centre of the altar, comes from the eleventh century, but was not a general usage till the sixteenth.

---

[1] The *Dies Irae* (thirteenth century) is an elaboration of the ninth Responsory (*Libera*) at Matins in the Office for the Dead, which is also used at funerals.

[2] Composed by St. Thomas Aquinas.

[3] The *domne* in this request is addressed to the celebrant and is used at High Mass. In a Low Mass the celebrant says the formula with *Domine*, addressed to God.

Munda cor meum . . .

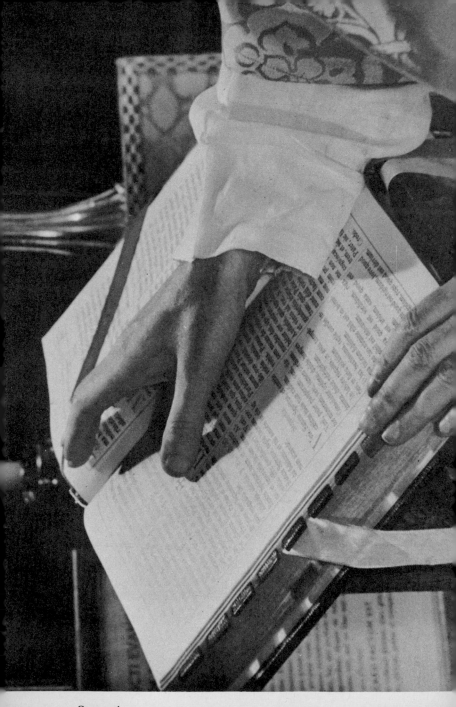

Sequentia . . .

GOSPEL

He goes to the Gospel side and says

S. Dominus vobiscum.
M. Et cum spiritu tuo.
S. Sequentia sancti Evangelii se-
cundum N.
M. Gloria tibi Domine.

P. The Lord be with you.
S. And with thy spirit.
P. The continuation of the holy
Gospel according to N.
S. Glory to Thee, O Lord.

At that time: There went forth a decree from Caesar Augustus . . . Glory to God in the highest; and on earth peace to men of good will (*Luke ii.* 1–14).

M. Laus tibi, Christe.

S. Praise to Thee, O Christ.

The priest kisses the book and says

S. Per evangelica dicta deleantur
nostra delicta.

P. Through the words of the
Gospel may our sins be blotted out.

Gospel. The Gospel Book, richly adorned, was the only thing in earlier times which was allowed to lie on the altar where the Body of Our Lord was to lie; the deacon still places it there during High Mass. Taken to represent Christ Himself, it was preceded by lighted candles to the Ambo (as now to the lectern at High Mass), and thus given the pomp of a full Entrance; at a stational Mass it had already been carried in procession from the Lateran. Candles, it must be noted, were carried before a *person*—as at the bishop's entrance and a High Mass entrance. The practice was taken from that of carrying lights before the Emperor. The candles carried before the celebrant at his entrance were eventually placed on the altar, in the eleventh century, and came in time to be connected with the Sacrament—so now we have candles on the altar as well.

The Gospel was sung from the summit of the Ambo, the Epistle often from its steps or from another Ambo. It is prefaced by *Dominus vobiscum . . . , Sequentia sancti evangelii . . .* (" The continuation of the holy gospel . . . "), which recalls the time when the Gospels were arranged to follow successively through the New Testament in a regular course. As he says these words the celebrant (the deacon at High Mass) makes a Sign of the Cross first on the open book and then on his forehead, lips (which are going to frame the words of the Gospel and which he has prayed to be cleansed) and breast. We first hear of the deacon and all the faithful signing themselves, at the deacon's announcement, in the ninth century; the full ritual of signing the book and then forehead, lips and breast is first attested in the eleventh. All this is a mark of the great reverence paid to the Gospel Book and, of course, to the Gospel itself, which is the climax of this part of the Mass. The server's reply here, *Gloria tibi Domine* (" Glory to Thee, O Lord "), and at the end of the Gospel, *Laus tibi Christe* (" Praise to Thee, O Christ "), are both connected with the idea of the Gospel Book representing Christ; these responses belonged to the assisting clergy and not to the people.

At the end of the Gospel the celebrant kisses the book and says silently, *Per evangelica dicta* (" Through the words of the Gospel . . . "). At the Pope's stational Mass in the seventh century all the clergy present kissed the book after him, and in Northern lands the faithful did so too—though for their kiss it was shut while the celebrant kissed it open at the place, as he still does. The practice of the clergy kissing the book lasted in some parts of France right up to the eighteenth century. Various formulas were used with the celebrant's kiss from the eleventh century; our own cannot be traced beyond the fifteenth.

(SERMON) then

Credo in unum Deum Patrem omnipotentem, factorem coeli et terrae, visibilium omnium, et invisibilium.

Et in unum Dominum Jesum Christum, Filium Dei unigenitum. Et ex Patre natum ante omnia saecula. Deum de Deo, lumen de lumine, Deum verum de Deo vero. Genitum, non factum, consubstantialem Patri: per quem omnia facta sunt.

I believe in one God the Father almighty, Maker of heaven and earth, and of all things visible and invisible.

And in one Lord Jesus Christ, the only-begotten Son of God, born of the Father before all ages; God of God, light of light, true God of true God; begotten not made, consubstantial with the Father, by whom all things were made. Who for us

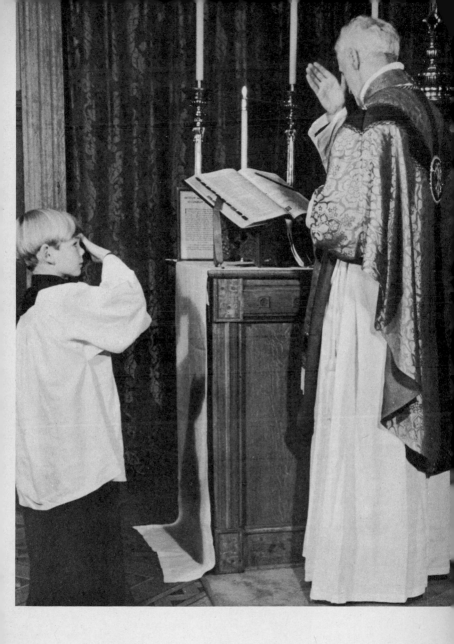

. . . sancti evangelii . . .

Credo . . . et homo factus est

Qui propter nos homines, et propter nostram salutem descendit de coelis. Et incarnatus est de Spiritu sancto ex Maria Virgine: ET HOMO FACTUS EST. Crucifixus etiam pro nobis: sub Pontio Pilato passus, et sepultus est. Et resurrexit tertia die, secundum Scripturas. Et ascendit in coelum: sedet ad dexteram Patris. Et iterum venturus est cum gloria judicare vivos et mortuos: cujus regni non erit finis.

Et in Spiritum sanctum, Dominum, et vivificantem: qui ex Patre, Filioque procedit. Qui cum Patre, et Filio simul adoratur, et conglorificatur: qui locutus est per Prophetas. Et unam sanctam catholicam et apostolicam Ecclesiam. Confiteor unum baptisma in remissionem peccatorum. Et exspecto resurrectionem mortuorum. Et vitam venturi saeculi. Amen.

men, and for our salvation, came down from heaven; and was incarnate by the Holy Ghost, of the Virgin Mary; AND WAS MADE MAN. He was crucified also for us, suffered under Pontius Pilate, and was buried. And the third day He rose again according to the Scriptures; and ascended into heaven, sitteth at the right hand of the Father; and He shall come again with glory to judge both the living and the dead; of whose kingdom there shall be no end.

And I believe in the Holy Ghost, the Lord and giver of life, who proceedeth from the Father and the Son; who together with the Father and the Son is adored and glorified; who spake by the prophets. And in one holy Catholic and apostolic Church. I confess one baptism for the remission of sins. And I look for the resurrection of the dead and the life of the world to come. Amen.

Credo. Though this profession of faith is usually called the Nicene Creed, it is not in fact the actual Creed drawn up by the Council of Nicea (325), but a conflation of the Creeds of Nicea and Constantinople (381). The preoccupation of these Councils with defining the doctrine of the Blessed Trinity in the face of various prevailing errors accounts for the semi-technical terms used. All such professions of faith derive their form from that used by the recipient of Baptism, and hence the singular, *Credo* ("I believe"). The Creed was very early transferred to the liturgy in the East, but only later in the West and not till the end of the tenth century at Rome, which maintained the proud claim of never having erred in the faith and so not needing an anti-heretical profession. When it was added to the Roman Mass, the rule was that the Creed should be used only on those occasions which its own formulas referred to—the feasts of those mysteries of the Incarnation mentioned (the Nativity, etc.), feasts of Our Lady, of the apostles (*apostolicam ecclesiam*), of All Saints (*sanctam ecclesiam*) and of the

88   THE BREAKING OF BREAD

consecration of a church. Now it is extended to Sundays and all greater feasts.[1]

OFFERTORY

S. Dominus vobiscum.
M. Et cum spiritu tuo.
S. Oremus.

P. The Lord be with you.
S. And with thy spirit.
P. Let us pray.

OFFERTORY CHANT

(Ps. xcv. 11, 13): Laetentur coeli et exsultet terra ante faciem Domini: quoniam venit.

Let the heavens rejoice and let the earth be glad before the face of the Lord: for He comes.

Dominus vobiscum. Oremus. Immediately after the Gospel (or Sermon and Creed when these occur) the priest makes this formal introduction to an *oratio*, which we have frequently encountered—and no *oratio* follows. Instead, he reads the Offertory chant, and we know it to have been a late practice that the priest should read this chant from the missal. One might explain this very unusual procedure by saying that the greeting and invitation to prayer is a vestige of the old Intercessory prayers which used to follow in the Synaxis at this place, and which still follow here on Good Friday, standing where the greeting at the opening of the Eucharist once stood, when this was still held apart from the Synaxis. This may well be part of the explanation, but there is another possibility—that the *action* of the Offertory, which symbolises our offering of ourselves, was considered so important as to need and justify this special call to prayer being made before it. And there is a still further factor: no *Dominus vobiscum* or *Oremus* precedes the Secret prayer (the prayer over the gifts) which concludes and brings to its climax the Offertory action, whereas all other formal *orationes* are introduced in this way. Is this call to

[1] It is also used on the feast of St. Mary Magdalen, some having called her the apostle to the apostles, as Our Lord sent her to bring them news of the Resurrection, others pointing to Our Lord's promise in Mark xiv. 9 (the Roman rite, unlike the Eastern rites, having always celebrated the feast of the " three Maries " as one).

Oremus before the Offertory

Suscipe sancte Pater

prayer the one belonging to the Secret? Rather a long time
ensues between them, but it is the time taken up by the action
of the Offertory during which there were no prayers prescribed for the celebrant to say until quite a late date.

Offertory chant. This space was, however, accompanied
or "covered" by the chant which we know to have been in use
at Rome at least from the fifth century. The name *Offertorium*
is attested from the seventh. It consisted of a psalm with antiphon, variable for the feast, but sometimes half the antiphon
was repeated after every verse (as in Responsory singing) to
make it last the required time; or the same effect was achieved
by musical embellishment of the chant. Not many of our
present Offertory chants have obvious relevance to the bringing
of gifts (as, e.g., at the Epiphany and Pentecost), owing to the
lapse of the Offertory procession and the consequent survival
of the antiphon alone. The chants in our missal for the Sundays
after Pentecost progress through the Book of Psalms step by
step with the other chants, but many of them are now taken
from other parts of the Bible with reference to a particular
feast or occasion, and show no attempt to refer to the bringing
of gifts.

The priest takes the paten with the host, which he offers up, saying

Suscipe, sancte Pater, omnipotens aeterne Deus, hanc immaculatam hostiam, quam ego indignus famulus tuus offero tibi Deo meo vivo et vero, pro innumerabilibus peccatis, et offensionibus, et neglegentiis meis, et pro omnibus circumstantibus, sed et pro omnibus fidelibus christianis vivis atque defunctis: ut mihi et illis proficiat ad salutem in vitam aeternam. Amen.

Receive, O holy Father, almighty and eternal God, this spotless host, which I, Thine unworthy servant, do offer unto Thee, my living and true God, for my many sins, my faults and my carelessness, and for all here present; as well as for all faithful Christians, living or dead; that it may help both me and them to obtain eternal life. Amen.

The priest pours wine and water into the chalice, saying

Deus, qui humanae substantiae dignitatem mirabiliter condidisti, et mirabilius reformasti: da nobis per

O God, who in creating human nature, hast wonderfully dignified it, and still more wonderfully reformed

hujus aquae et vini mysterium, ejus divinitatis esse consortes, qui humanitatis nostrae fieri dignatus est particeps, Jesus Christus Filius tuus Dominus noster: Qui tecum vivit et regnat in unitate Spiritus sancti Deus: per omnia saecula saeculorum. Amen.

it; grant that by the mystery of this water and wine, we may be made partakers of His divine nature, who vouchsafed to become partaker of our human nature, even Jesus Christ Thy Son Our Lord; who with Thee, in the unity of the Holy Ghost, etc. Amen.

Then he takes the chalice, and offers it, saying

Offerimus tibi, Domine, calicem salutaris, tuam deprecantes clementiam: ut in conspectu divinae majestatis tuae, pro nostra, et totius mundi salute cum odore suavitatis ascendat. Amen.

We offer unto Thee, O Lord, the chalice of salvation, beseeching Thy clemency, that it may ascend before Thy divine Majesty, as a sweet odour, for our salvation and for that of the whole world. Amen.

Then, bowing down, he says

In spiritu humilitatis, et in animo contrito suscipiamur a te, Domine; et sic fiat sacrificium nostrum in conspectu tuo hodie, ut placeat tibi, Domine Deus.

Accept us, O Lord, in the spirit of humility and contrition of heart: and grant that the sacrifice we offer this day in Thy sight, may be pleasing to Thee, O Lord God.

Then he makes the sign of the Cross over the host and chalice, saying

Veni sanctificator omnipotens et aeterne Deus: et benedic hoc sacrificium, tuo sancto nomini praeparatum.

Come, O almighty and eternal God, the sanctifier, and bless this sacrifice, prepared for the glory of Thy holy name.

He washes his hands, saying

Lavabo inter innocentes manus meas: et circumdabo altare tuum, Domine.

Ut audiam vocem laudis: et enarrem universa mirabilia tua.

Domine, dilexi decorem domus tuae: et locum habitationis gloriae tuae.

Ne perdas cum impiis, Deus, animam meam: et cum viris sanguinum vitam meam.

In quorum manibus iniquitates sunt: dextera eorum repleta est muneribus.

Ego autem in innocentia mea ingressus sum: redime me, et miserere mei.

Pes meus stetit in directo: in ecclesiis benedicam te, Domine.

Gloria Patri . . .

I will wash my hands among the innocent; and will compass Thy altar, O Lord.

That I may hear the voice of Thy praise, and tell all Thy wondrous works.

I have loved, O Lord, the beauty of Thy house, and the place where Thy glory dwelleth.

Take not away my soul, O God, with the wicked, nor my life with bloody men.

In whose hands are iniquities: their right hand is filled with gifts.

But I have walked in my innocence: redeem me, and have mercy on me.

My foot hath stood in the direct way; in the churches I will bless Thee, O Lord.

Glory be to the Father . . .

Then at the centre of the altar he says

Suscipe sancta Trinitas hanc oblationem, quam tibi offerimus ob memoriam passionis, resurrectionis, et ascensionis Jesu Christi Domini nostri: et in honorem beatae Mariae semper Virginis, et beati Joannis Baptistae et sanctorum Apostolorum Petri et Pauli, et istorum, et omnium Sanctorum: ut illis proficiat ad honorem, nobis autem ad salutem: et illi pro nobis intercedere dignentur in coelis, quorum memoriam agimus in terris. Per eumdem Christum Dominum nostrum. Amen.

Receive, O holy Trinity, this oblation which we make to Thee in memory of the Passion, Resurrection and Ascension of our Lord Jesus Christ, and in honour of the blessed Mary, ever a Virgin, of blessed John Baptist, the holy apostles Peter and Paul, and of all the saints; that it may be available to their honour, and our salvation; and that they may vouchsafe to intercede for us in heaven, whose memory we celebrate on earth. Through the same Christ our Lord. Amen.

Priest's prayers at the Offertory. With the growth of private Masses and the general tendency to fill in the "gaps" when the priest was saying nothing, we find, particularly in Gallican lands from where the custom spread, a number of "private" prayers coming into use during the Middle Ages. These prayers arise from two ideas in particular: the offering by the priest of *his own gift*, his own contribution to the sacrifice; and the various *intentions* for which his and other people's gifts were being offered. It is true of all of them to say that their ancestry or outline can be traced back to the eighth or ninth centuries, but that the precise wording now in use represents a final form to which they had developed by the end of the Middle Ages.

Suscipe sancte Pater and **Offerimus** (" Receive, O Holy Father . . . " and " We offer unto Thee . . . "), which the priest says as he offers host and chalice respectively, are two from a number of medieval formulas in use during the celebrant's offering of his own gift; such formulas were variable at their first appearance, the celebrant voicing the intentions he chose, but eventually came to have a fixed wording and to cover all the intentions in general terms. At first the chalice was filled with wine, and the water mixed with it, before the beginning of Mass, and it was the deacon's task to bring up the chalice at the Offertory. The *Offerimus*, when introduced, was said by the deacon in the priest's name; later the priest said it with him, and so it is worded in the plural whereas the *Suscipe sancte Pater* is in the singular. At High Mass now the deacon puts the wine and water into the chalice and priest and deacon say the *Offerimus* together.

In the Eastern rites the ritual of laying ready the bread to be consecrated is a very complicated one, several particles being used and arranged in a special way. In the West too, when all the hosts for Communion would be laid on the altar at the Offertory, this ritual had included laying the particles in the form of a cross; a relic of this is to be found in the Sign of the Cross which the priest makes with host and chalice, after he has offered each to God, and before laying them on the corporal.

Deus qui humanae substantiae (" O God, who in creating human nature . . . ") is now said between the offering of host and chalice, for it was natural for a formula to come into use for the mixing of water with the wine, as soon as this began to be done at the altar and during the Offertory. The act itself had always been vested with great significance. Our Lord would have used, and consecrated, wine mixed with water at the Last Supper, and from the earliest extant writings of the Church this water has been taken to represent *us*; the small quantity of water becomes merged with the wine and so transformed into the Blood of Christ, even as by the Eucharist we ourselves are to be changed spiritually into Christ. The *Deus qui humanae substantiae* is an old Roman Christmas Collect, with the words *aquae et vini* inserted into it (" by this mystery *of water and wine* "): the very bold plea that we be made " partakers of his divinity " echoes 2 Pet. i. 4. Because of its significance, the water put in is blessed in the course of this prayer.

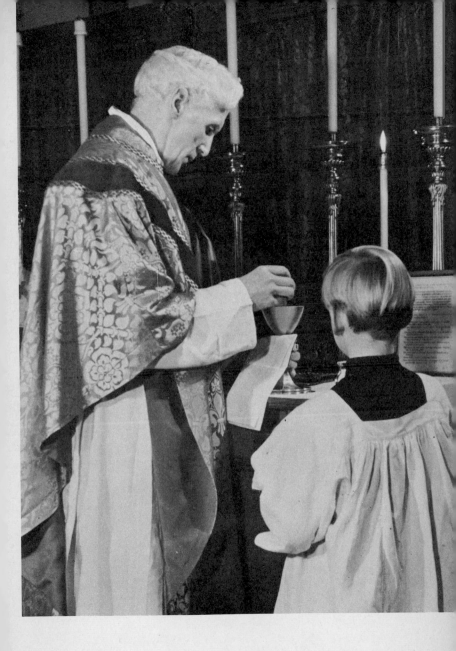

Pouring in the wine

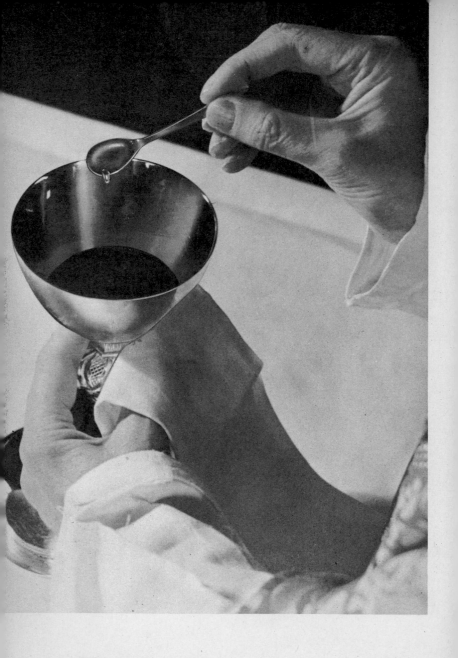

The drop of water

Raising the chalice for the offering

Veni sanctificator . . . et benedic

In spiritu humilitatis comes next in our Mass, but an account of it is more conveniently given later, with that of the *Suscipe sancta Trinitas*.

Veni sanctificator (" Come, O almighty and eternal God . . . "). The Middle Ages was the age of blessings and it was natural that the gifts, when prepared and offered, should be blessed. This formula is one of the prayers then in use for such a blessing and is addressed to the Holy Spirit, the Sanctifier, the invocation of whom plays a much more important role in the Eastern rites. It is accompanied here by a gesture expressive of petition for a blessing which is also used at the *Te igitur* (the words of which are similar to those of this prayer) and at the Blessing proper at the end of Mass, *Benedicat vos*: this gesture —of opening, raising and rejoining the hands in a wide circle— is followed by a Sign of the Cross over host and chalice.

Lavabo. We have already noted that hand-washing, as a sign of purifying the intention and of banishing the cares and preoccupations of daily life, was a very old Christian practice of Jewish origin. The hand-washing of the priest before vesting, the *Asperges* before the sung Mass on Sundays and the holy water stoups at the entrance to the church are all expressions of the same idea. It was introduced here as a practical necessity after the handling of the offerings (and incense), but never lost its symbolic meaning as an act of reverence towards the sacred elements about to be handled during the Canon; our present pouring of water over the finger-tips has this purely symbolic value. Ps. xxv. 6–12, *Lavabo* (" I will wash my hands . . . "), first appeared in the Middle Ages accompanying the priest's hand-washing before vesting and was later moved to this place.

Suscipe sancta Trinitas (" Receive, O holy Trinity, . . ."). With this prayer and the *In spiritu humilitatis* (" Accept us, O Lord, . . . ") we have an instance of the Roman Mass including two of a set of *alternative* formulas expressing the same ideas.[1] Both prayers are said in the same posture—the priest bowing before the centre of the altar with his joined hands just resting on its edge—which is one of supplication, and of asking God to receive our offering; the same gesture accompanying the same ideas occurs in the Canon prayers *Te igitur* and *Supplices*; and in all four there is similarity of wording. The *Suscipe sancta Trinitas* was said after the Offertory procession and was a formula for expressing the intentions of those who had brought the offerings, so that its contents could vary. But from being a formula coming at the beginning of the statement of intentions it became one summing them up, worded in general terms and coming at the end. The content of the prayer as it eventually developed shows two borrowings from the Canon: there is the " remembrance of the passion, resurrection and ascension of Our Lord Jesus Christ " as in the chief prayer of offering in the Canon; and the intercession of Our Lady, St. John the Baptist, the apostles and all saints is invoked as in *Communicantes*, etc.

Orate fratres: ut meum ac vestrum sacrificium acceptabile fiat apud Deum Patrem omnipotentem.
M. Suscipiat Dominus sacrificium de manibus tuis ad laudem et gloriam nominis sui, ad utilitatem quoque nostram, totiusque Ecclesiae suae sanctae.
S. Amen.

Brethren, pray that my sacrifice and yours may be acceptable to God the Father almighty.
S. May the Lord receive the sacrifice from thy hands, to the praise and glory of His name, and to our benefit, and that of all His holy Church.
P. Amen.

SECRET PRAYER(S)

Accepta tibi sit, Domine, quae-sumus, hodiernae festivitatis oblatio: ut, tua gratia largiente, per haec

Let the offering of this day's festival be acceptable to Thee, O Lord, we beseech Thee; that by Thy

[1] The *In spiritu humilitatis* is an Anglo-Saxon prayer, taking the place in the Anglo-Saxon liturgy of the *Suscipe sancta Trinitas*.

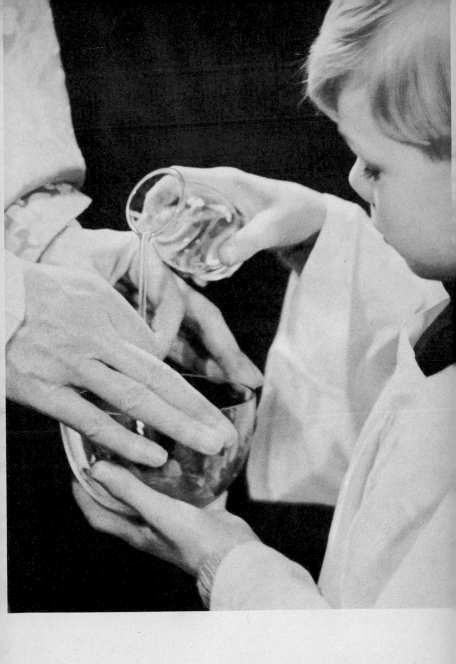

Lavabo inter innocentes . . .

Orate fratres . . .

sacrosancta commercia, in illius inveniamur forma, in quo tecum est nostra substantia: Qui tecum . . .

grace, through this sacred exchange, we may be found like unto Him in whom our substance is united with Thee, who liveth and reigneth with Thee . . .

(aloud)

per omnia saecula saeculorum.
M. Amen.

for ever and ever.
S. Amen.

Orate fratres (" Brethren, pray . . . "). All the gifts being now prepared, the priest is going to speak solemnly in the name of the people (in the Secret) and then begin the Eucharistic Prayer, which is the very substance and kernel of his priestly action. The *Orate fratres* is a preliminary to this, asking us to pray that the sacrifice we have prepared and are now going to offer will be pleasing to God. It is really a more elaborate form of the *Oremus* or of *Sursum corda* (" Lift up your hearts ") and was first addressed to the clergy assisting[1] (*fratres*), though soon extended to everyone so that some of the earlier forms have *fratres et sorores* (" brothers and sisters "). Such a prayer is found in the early Middle Ages in both East and West, and took various forms: the precise form we now use became fixed in the twelfth century. At first there was no answer to the *Orate fratres*—and there still is none on Good Friday when, after the Synaxis rite[2] and veneration of the cross, there takes place a simple Communion service (not a Mass, as there is no Consecration) which shows many of the characteristics of the early ritual before the medieval developments were introduced, as we shall indicate in their place. Answers, however, to the *Orate fratres*, made by the clergy, appear quite early, from the ninth century; our own *Suscipiat* (" May the Lord receive . . .") was quite a regular answer in the eleventh, at least in Italy. The fact that at the *Orate fratres* the priest turns fully round, clockwise, whereas at *Dominus vobiscum*, etc., he turns to face the

[1] This explains the rubric that it should be said " in a slightly raised voice ", less loudly than the other parts said aloud; cf. the three words *Nobis quoque peccatoribus*, p. 139.

[2] See p. 28.

congregation and then turns back the same way, has apparently no more profound explanation than the position of the missal, to which he is next going to turn.

The Secret. The practice of saying this " prayer over the gifts " inaudibly seems to have come to Rome from beyond the Alps in about the eighth century, very shortly before the custom of the silent Canon came by the same route. The prayers, which vary with the feast, usually mention our gifts, offerings, victims, sacrifice; and they often express the realisation that our own gifts do not by themselves constitute a sacrifice, by asking God to " sanctify ", to consecrate, them— i.e. to take them up into the sacrifice of Christ. There is always some petition in the Secret, which is thus formed on the pattern of the Collect; and the Roman Secrets are even more terse in their expression than the Collects in the same rite.

EUCHARISTIC PRAYER

DIALOGUE

S. Dominus vobiscum.
M. Et cum spiritu tuo.

P. The Lord be with you.
S. And with thy spirit.

S. Sursum corda.
M. Habemus ad Dominum.

P. Lift up your hearts.
S. We lift them up to the Lord.

S. Gratias agamus Domino Deo nostro.
M. Dignum et justum est.

P. Let us give thanks to the Lord our God.
S. It is meet and just.

THE (COMMON) PREFACE

Vere dignum et justum est, aequum et salutare, nos tibi semper, et ubique gratias agere: Domine sancte, Pater omnipotens, aeterne Deus: per Christum Dominum nostrum. Per quem majestatem tuam laudant Angeli, adorant Dominationes, tremunt Potestates. Coeli, coelorumque Virtutes, ac beata Seraphim, socia exsultatione concelebrant. Cum quibus et nostras voces, ut admitti jubeas, deprecamur, supplici confessione dicentes:

It is indeed right and fitting, just and availing unto salvation that we should at all times and in all places give thanks to Thee, holy Lord, Father almighty, eternal God: through Christ our Lord. Through whom the angels praise, the dominations worship, the powers reverence Thy majesty: the heavens, and the heavenly hosts, and the blessed seraphim are united in joyful celebration. To their voices, we pray Thee, let ours be added, while we say with humble praise:

Secret

Gratias agamus Domino Deo nostro

Sanctus, sanctus, sanctus, Dominus Deus Sabaoth. Pleni sunt coeli et terra gloria tua. Hosanna in excelsis. Benedictus qui venit in nomine Domini. Hosanna in excelsis.

Holy, Holy, Holy, Lord God of Hosts. Heaven and earth are full of Thy glory. Hosanna in the highest. Blessed is he that cometh in the name of the Lord. Hosanna in the highest.

Preface. This name, *praefatio* (opening speech), was first applied to the Dialogue which begins the Eucharistic Prayer; only later was it misunderstood as "preliminary introduction" and applied to the opening *Vere dignum* formulas, since the variability of these stood in marked contrast to the fixed contents of the rest of the Eucharistic Prayer. The result was that the Prefaces ceased to be thought of as part of that Prayer. In this opening dialogue, though it begins with *Dominus vobiscum*, the priest does not turn to greet the people as the dialogue was always part of the Prayer itself, and the priest and people pray together as one throughout.

The Common Preface is really the bare form of the Roman Prefaces without any special thanksgiving inserted or mystery commemorated. The list of thanksgivings in the Jewish thanksgiving-blessing dwelt at some length on God's gifts in creation and then went on to narrate some of His special care of the Jews as related in their sacred history. The Christian Eucharistic Prayer comes very soon to the phrase *per Christum Dominum nostrum*—almost at once in the Common Preface, whereas the others lead up to it by some account of Christian "sacred history"; while the earlier forms of the Prayer included all that was to be mentioned under this head, the Roman Prefaces are alternative ways of beginning the Prayer, each of which mentions just that particular mystery of Our Lord's life which is seasonable. At first we find different Prefaces for each Mass, and there are 267 of them in the earliest Roman sacramentary. Each one dwelt on the particular feast of the day, e.g. of a martyr, as something to thank God for, but they tended to become so elaborate in their description of the historical details

connected with the feast as to stray very far from the fundamental ideas of the Eucharistic Prayer and even to obscure
them. Reform came with Gregory I (c. 600), who seems to have
cut them down to fourteen, and of these seven later fell into
disuse, leaving only those for Christmas, Epiphany, Easter,
Ascension, Pentecost, the Apostles and the Common Preface
(for all other saints). By the eleventh century those of the Cross,
the Trinity, Our Lady and the Preface for Lent had been added,
making eleven in all; and so matters remained till the twentieth
century. Recent additions have been the Preface for the Dead
(1919), St. Joseph (1919), Christ the King (1925) and the
Sacred Heart (1928). The Common Preface was used for
Sundays till the thirteenth century, when the Gallican rite
started using the Preface for the Trinity, a practice not adopted
at Rome till the eighteenth century.

Sanctus and **Benedictus.** The idea that our praise and
adoration of God is joined to that of the angels, which is found
already in the Old Testament and St. Paul's Epistles, comes
into prominence towards the end of the Preface, and leads up
to the *Sanctus*. The description of the angelic praise can be
seen already in the earliest examples of the Eucharistic Prayer,
and so it is a primitive element, possibly Jewish in origin. It is
worthy of note that in the Prefaces the angelic worship is said
to ascend to God "through Christ". "Holy, holy, holy . . . of
Thy glory" is quoted from Isa. vi. 3, where it is the song of
the Seraphim. In the liturgy, at least in some places, this
Sanctus was an acclamation sung by the people in the same
simple tone as the one in which the Preface was intoned by the
priest, who introduced this cry by the concluding phrases of
the Preface ("our voices . . ."). It was first taken over from the
people by the assistant clergy (the deacon and subdeacon still
say it with the priest at High Mass), probably when both the
Latin and the chant became unfamiliar to the people; and

finally it was relegated to the choir. It is uncertain whether the *Sanctus* was included in the Mass quite as early as the description of the angelic worship,[1] but it was in use at least outside the Eucharist in the first century and may go back to the worship of the synagogue.

Hosanna . . . Benedictus ("Hosanna in the highest. Blessed is He . . ."), first appearing in the Gallican rite, was in use at Rome at least by the seventh century. It is from Ps. cxvii. 25, the Easter psalm, which was among those recited at the Last Supper and elsewhere in the Paschal ritual; it was with this verse of the psalm that Our Lord's triumphal entry into Jerusalem on Palm Sunday was greeted (Matt. xxi. 9), in recognition that He was King and Messiah. *Hosanna* is a Hebrew word, literally meaning "save, we pray", which had come to have a general sense of "Hurrah!" So the people cried out to Our Lord, "Hurrah for the son of David!" Both *Hosannas* really belong to the *Benedictus*, one before and one after, though we now sing one as a conclusion to the *Sanctus* for the sake of symmetry. Matt. xxi. 9 has: "Hosanna to the son of David: Blessed is He that cometh in the name of the Lord: Hosanna in the highest." The phrase "in the highest", which here balances "to the son of David", seems to involve a mistranslation of the Jewish preposition, and we should read: "Salvation to the son of David . . . salvation *from* on high"— i.e. a prayer for God's power and majesty to descend on the person hailed by the acclamation.

The musical embellishment of the *Sanctus* led to its lasting till the Elevation, and so the *Benedictus* came to be sung after the Elevation; the result is that now in High Mass the whole Eucharistic Prayer is accompanied by this twofold acclamation.

[1] It was used in Eastern liturgy earlier than in Western and came to Rome later than elsewhere in the West.

THE CANON

Te igitur, clementissime Pater, per Jesum Christum Filium tuum, Dominum nostrum, supplices rogamus ac petimus uti accepta habeas, et benedicas, haec dona, haec munera, haec sancta sacrificia illibata, in primis, quae tibi offerimus pro Ecclesia tua sancta catholica: quam pacificare, custodire, adunare, et regere digneris toto orbe terrarum: una cum famulo tuo Papa nostro N. et Antistite nostro N. et omnibus orthodoxis, atque catholicae et apostolicae fidei cultoribus.

We therefore humbly pray and beseech Thee, most merciful Father, through Jesus Christ, Thy Son, our Lord, that Thou wouldst vouchsafe to accept and bless these gifts, these presents, these holy unspotted sacrifices, which in the first place we offer Thee for Thy holy Catholic Church, to which vouchsafe to grant peace, as also to preserve, unite, and govern it throughout the world: together with thy servant N. our Pope, N. our Bishop, as also all orthodox believers and professors of the Catholic and apostolic faith.

The Canon. We are, perhaps, accustomed, from the arrangement of our prayer-books, to think of the Ordinary of the Mass as everything up to the Preface, and the Canon as everything after it. In fact, of course, the Canon is part of the Ordinary, i.e. of the invariable part of the Mass. "Canon" means formula, the Formula of the Eucharistic Prayer (*canon actionis*), which really begins with the Preface. But the variability of the Preface made people think of the Canon (the invariable Formula) as beginning after it, and hence of the Eucharistic Prayer as starting at *Te igitur*. This was helped by two other factors. The Preface was said or sung aloud and ended with an acclamation; the practice of saying the rest of the Eucharistic Prayer inaudibly came to Rome, via the Gallican rite, in the ninth century, and with it the break between the Preface and what follows became more marked. The Prayer, now regarded as beginning with *Te igitur*, was henceforth a "holy of holies" into which the priest, like the high priest of Judaism, though he entered in the name of the whole people, entered alone. A second factor is that we find the manuscripts, which at first run straight on, beginning to signalise the break by illuminating and decorating the "T" of *Te igitur*; it became customary to work it into a crucifix; and now a full-page picture of Calvary

Sanctus

Te igitur . . . supplices rogamus

appears in our missals between Preface and "Canon". The Canon really ends with the *Amen* before the *Pater Noster*, but the use of the word was gradually extended to all the rest of the invariable part of the Mass.

Those used to reading a Latin missal will have noticed the rubric *Infra actionem* (in red) before the *Communicantes*. In "pagan" Latin the word *agere* (to do) had come to have the sense of "to sacrifice", and *Actio* (or *actio sacra*) is one of the oldest Latin names for the Mass or for the Eucharistic Prayer. The rubric *infra actionem* occurs in some of the earliest Mass-books in the Propers of Masses to indicate that the group of prayers which follows is to be included in the Eucharistic Prayer.

Te igitur ("We therefore humbly pray . . ."). The fact that this prayer begins "Therefore . . ." is itself a sufficient indication that it is not a real beginning but takes up the Eucharist, the Act of Thanksgiving, which has already been begun in the Preface. "It is meet and just that we should give thanks . . . through Christ Our Lord . . . Therefore. . . .": these are the leading ideas so far in the Eucharistic Prayer.

The *Te igitur* is a petition for the acceptance of our offering. The prayer is something of a mystery, because quite unparalleled in other rites, but it is highly probable that already by the end of the fourth century the Roman Canon passed from the "thanksgiving" thought of the Preface via *some* form of prayer for the acceptance of our offering straight to the *Quam oblationem* ("Which offering . . ."—i.e. the offering having already been mentioned), and so to the words of consecration.[1] This clear transition was broken by the insertion of the Names and prayers of intercession. Only if we realise how closely the idea of Christian thanksgiving was linked to that of offering, can we

---

[1] Formulas unmistakably like the *Te igitur* are known from the fifth century (and may be earlier), but at different places in the Canon.

understand the sequence of thought: *oblatio* (offering) is the earliest Latin translation the Christians used for the Greek word *eucharistia* (thanksgiving): thus it was perfectly natural, a development of the same thought, to pray: *Vere dignum* (it is right that we should give thanks); *Te igitur* (therefore we ask you to receive our offering); *Quam oblationem* (which offering . . .).

The gesture of bowing here and in the *Supplices* at the words *supplices rogamus* ("We humbly beseech") has already been noted above where it occurs in the Offertory. The idea of making a humble prayer for the acceptance of our sacrifice does not involve any doubt whether the offering of Our Lord's Body and Blood will be acceptable to God; He was accepted once for all in His Ascension, when He was received "at the right hand of God", and is a Victim eternally acceptable. Rather, it is the consciousness that *our* gifts and in a true sense *ourselves*—represented by our gifts—are to be transformed into Christ and *so* offered to God, that prompts this prayer for acceptance and the recurrence of the same idea in other prayers.

A further gesture that occurs in the *Te igitur* and elsewhere in the Canon is the Sign of the Cross which the priest makes three times over the *oblata*. The three crosses here are the oldest in the Canon, attested from the eighth century, and it is from here that the gesture seems to have spread to other places. The Sign of the Cross as a blessing comes from the Gallican rite, the old Roman (originally Jewish) form of blessing being to extend the hands over the object to be blessed. In the earliest (third century) document giving the Roman rite in any detail we find that the bishop says the whole Eucharistic Prayer with his hands extended over the *oblata*, and this gesture is preserved during our *Hanc igitur* ("We therefore beseech Thee . . ."). The crosses are always closely connected with such words as "bless", "sanctify", etc., or with any reference to the gifts, offerings. In this latter case they seem to be gestures of offering—an indication by the hands of the gifts we mention. We must recall again the close mental connection in early times between blessing and thanksgiving (the thanksgiving-blessing) and between thanksgiving and offering.

When first dealing with the Canon[1] we noted that the petitions of the Intercessory Prayers had been introduced into the Canon from their old place at the end of the Synaxis (except on Good Friday, when there is no Eucharistic Prayer), with the idea that all our petitions will be more effective if incorporated into "The Prayer" (*prex*) of the Church. So here in the *Te igitur* we meet with something new at the words *in primis* ("in the first place"): we begin the list of intercessions, the expression of our intentions within the Canon. Already appearing in the Eastern Canon early in the fourth century, the intercessions are introduced at Rome before the end of it. We pray first and foremost (*in primis*) for the Church herself, and then begin the Names. The prayer for *orthodoxis atque . . . cultoribus*[2] is really a prayer for all bishops who are in communion with the Church, i.e. not heretics, and not for "all orthodox believers"—these come in later; the bishops are given the twofold name, theological and biblical, of "right-thinking . . . tillers" of the Lord's vineyard.

Memento, Domine, famulorum famularumque tuarum N. et N. Et omnium circumstantium, quorum tibi fides cognita est, et nota devotio, pro quibus tibi offerimus: vel qui tibi offerunt hoc sacrificium laudis, pro se, suisque omnibus: pro redemptione animarum suarum, pro spe salutis, et incolumitatis suae: tibique reddunt vota sua aeterno Deo, vivo et vero.

Be mindful, O Lord, of Thy servants, men and women, N. and N. And of all here present, whose faith and devotion are known unto Thee, for whom we offer, or who offer up to Thee this sacrifice of praise for themselves, their families and friends, for the redemption of their souls, for the health and salvation they hope for, and for which they now pay their vows to Thee, the eternal, living and true God.

Communicantes, et memoriam venerantes, in primis gloriosae semper Virginis Mariae, Genitricis Dei

Communicating with, and honouring in the first place, the memory of the glorious and ever-Virgin Mary,

[1] See p. 42.
[2] The phrase is post-Gregorian and non-Roman.

et Domini nostri Jesu Christi: sed et beatorum Apostolorum ac Martyrum tuorum, Petri et Pauli, Andreae, Jacobi, Joannis, Thomae, Jacobi, Philippi, Bartholomaei, Matthaei, Simonis et Thaddaei, Lini, Cleti, Clementis, Xysti, Cornelii, Cypriani, Laurentii, Chrysogoni, Joannis et Pauli, Cosmae et Damiani: et omnium Sanctorum tuorum; quorum meritis precibusque concedas, ut in omnibus protectionis tuae muniamur auxilio. Per eumdem Christum Dominum nostrum. Amen.

Mother of our Lord and God Jesus Christ; as also of the blessed Apostles and Martyrs, Peter and Paul, Andrew, James, John, Thomas, James, Philip, Bartholomew, Matthew, Simon and Thaddeus, Linus, Cletus, Clement, Xystus, Cornelius, Cyprian, Lawrence, Chrysogonus, John and Paul, Cosmas and Damian, and of all Thy saints; through whose merits and prayers grant that we may be always defended by the help of Thy protection. Through the same Christ our Lord. Amen.

Memento Domine ("Be mindful, O Lord, . . ."). At least in the West the naming of the living was introduced well before any mention of the dead, whether the "great dead" (the saints) or our own personal dead. After the pastors of the Church are named those of us here present at this Mass *qui tibi offerunt* ("who offer up to Thee"). It seems that the priest used to pause in silence while another cleric read the names of those present who for some reason were specially to be prayed for (e.g. particular benefactors).[1] The pause came before the mention of "all here present", *circumstantium*, who are described as standing round the altar, as they would be in the earlier churches. The pause still comes before the general formula referring to those present, but during it we all pray for our living relatives and friends according to our own choice.

There is one oddity in this prayer. The phrase *pro quibus tibi offerimus, vel* ("*for whom we offer, or* who offer up to Thee") first appears in the tenth century. It is an *alternative* to the phrase "who offer up to Thee", to be used according as those who had made the offering for the Mass were present among the *circumstantes* or not; if they were not present, the priest would say, "for whom we (who are present) offer", meaning "in their stead" or "for their intention", and not meaning that the Mass was being "offered for" them.

[1] It was an Eastern and Gallican usage to read the names of those who had made a ritual offering of bread and wine.

Memento for the living

Hanc igitur . . .

The phrases "sacrifice of praise . . . pay their vows" are taken from Ps. xlix. 14; "the living and true God" from 1 Thess. i. 9, the Christians making clear that their sacrifice is different from the pagan sacrifices which are offered to lifeless and false gods. The second half of the prayer couches in general terms the intentions we would have in our minds when praying for living persons, *salus* looking rather to the salvation of their souls, *incolumitas* to their bodily welfare.

Communicantes. This first word, "communicating", is rather up in the air as it stands, and it is not at once clear with what noun the participle agrees. The oldest texts read *tibi reddunt*, "they pay to Thee", (and not "and who pay to Thee"), at the close of the previous prayer: these words, therefore, begin a new sentence, "they pay their vows to Thee", to the subject of which the two participles, "communicating and reverencing the memory", are attached. It seems likely, then, that the word *communicantes* should be construed with what comes immediately before, "communicating with the one true God". But many other explanations have been given.

The saints named in our prayer show a careful arrangement, which dates from the end of the sixth century. We have Our Lady followed by twelve apostles and twelve martyrs; the latter are arranged hierarchically, there being six bishops of whom the first five are Popes, then two clerics (Lawrence, Chrysogonus[1]) and four laymen (John and Paul, Cosmas and Damian). The list of apostles differs in its order of names from all other known lists and may be arranged thus for its assonance. The list of martyrs contains the names of those whom we know to have been venerated at Rome by the end of the sixth century.

At the end of the prayer we find a closing formula, *Per Christum Dominum nostrum*, which has the effect of making this an isolated prayer and breaking up the unity of the Eucharistic

---

[1] In fact nothing is known of Chrysogonus, but legend made him a cleric.

Prayer. The same formula occurs, with the same effect, after *Hanc igitur*, *Supplices* and the *Memento* for the Dead, and after *Nobis quoque peccatoribus* we have it without any concluding *Amen*. In fact the formula is not a closing formula, but a taking-up and repetition of the *Per Christum Dominum nostrum* which occurs half-way through the Preface; this idea, that all our prayer is through Christ, is kept constantly in mind before the Consecration in order to lead to the narrative of Our Lord's institution of the Eucharist, and after the Consecration in order to lead up to the great doxology, *Per ipsum*. . . . It is only in the ninth century that an *Amen* begins to be added to these formulas by analogy with the closing formulas of other prayers. There is really only place for one closing formula, the great doxology itself and the people's *Amen*.

Hanc igitur oblationem servitutis nostrae, sed et cunctae familiae tuae, quaesumus, Domine, ut placatus accipias: diesque nostros in tua pace disponas, atque ab aeterna damnatione nos eripi, et in electorum tuorum jubeas grege numerari. Per Christum Dominum nostrum. Amen.

We therefore pray Thee, O Lord, mercifully to accept this offering of our service and that of all Thy family: to order our days in Thy peace, and to deliver us from eternal damnation and to number us in the flock of Thine elect. Through Christ our Lord. Amen.

Hanc igitur. This prayer seems at first sight to be another form of Prayer for Acceptance, like the *Te igitur*. In its present form it derives from the close of the sixth century, but the fact that before this time it is found in a great variety of forms indicates that it was a variable formula for expressing the particular intentions for which the Mass was being offered. When we offer a Mass now for particular persons, we mention their names privately at the Commemoration of the living or dead; but we have seen that the *Memento* for the living was originally intended for mentioning the names of those present who were offering the Mass, and not for expressing the intentions for which it was being offered. Hence a formula arose for this purpose, with a variable content; but the variety of such contents tended to obscure the Eucharistic Prayer and particularise the sacrifice, so a general formula, the *Hanc igitur*, was introduced to sum up our intentions in general terms.

Quam oblationem tu Deus in omnibus, quaesumus, benedictam, adscriptam, ratam, rationabilem, acceptabilemque facere digneris; ut nobis Corpus et Sanguis fiat dilectissimi Filii tui Domini nostri Jesu Christi.

Which oblation do Thou, O God, vouchsafe in all respects to make blessed, approved, ratified, reasonable and acceptable; that it may be made for us the Body and Blood of Thy most beloved Son Jesus Christ our Lord.

Quam oblationem. This prayer forms a transition to the institution-narrative. In the earliest form in which we meet it, in the fourth century, it is a prayer *for* the Consecration, which is just about to follow. By the sixth century, to which our present form belongs, it has undergone a change: the petition is now that our offering may have been duly performed, our sacrifice correctly prepared, in order that the Transformation may follow (*ut nobis fiat . . .*). Our worship of God is called *rationabile* (reasonable, spiritual) by St. Paul (Rom. xii. 1), but the word as used here has, already in the earlier form of the prayer, come to mean "in due form", and is surrounded by words of a similarly legal flavour; *adscriptam* means in secular contexts something like "entered on the rolls"—so here, "ratified" by God, recognised by Him.

Qui pridie quam pateretur, accepit panem in sanctas, ac venerabiles manus suas, et elevatis oculis in coelum ad te Deum Patrem suum omnipotentem, tibi gratias agens, benedixit, fregit, deditque discipulis suis, dicens: Accipite, et manducate ex hoc omnes, HOC EST ENIM CORPUS MEUM.

Who the day before He suffered took bread into His holy and venerable hands, and with His eyes lifted up towards heaven, giving thanks to Thee, almighty God, His Father, He blessed it, brake it, and gave it to His disciples, saying: Take ye all and eat of this, FOR THIS IS MY BODY.

Elevation of the Host

Simili modo postquam coenatum est, accipiens et hunc praeclarum Calicem in sanctas ac venerabiles manus suas: item tibi gratias agens, benedixit, deditque discipulis suis, dicens: Accipite, et bibite ex eo

In like manner, after He had supped, taking this excellent Chalice into His holy and venerable hands, giving Thee also thanks, He blessed, and gave it to His disciples, saying: Take ye all and drink of this, FOR

omnes. HIC EST ENIM CALIX SAN-
GUINIS MEI, NOVI ET AETERNI TESTA-
MENTI: MYSTERIUM FIDEI: QUI PRO
VOBIS ET PRO MULTIS EFFUNDETUR IN
REMISSIONEM PECCATORUM.

THIS IS THE CHALICE OF MY BLOOD
OF THE NEW AND ETERNAL TESTA-
MENT: THE MYSTERY OF FAITH:
WHICH SHALL BE SHED FOR YOU, AND
FOR MANY, TO THE REMISSION OF SINS.

Haec quotiescumque feceritis, in
mei memoriam facietis.

As often as you shall do these
things, you shall do them in memory
of Me.

Elevation of the chalice

Qui pridie. With this we come to the institution-narrative
and Consecration, the kernel of the liturgies. The liturgical
texts of this account of the Last Supper are not the same in
their wording as the New Testament texts[1] and show two ten-
dencies—to make the account of the consecration of the Bread
parallel with that of the consecration of the Wine; and to add
theological explanatory phrases. In this respect the Roman
text is less elaborated than many others and may well go back
to more ancient times. One example of this kind of elaboration
is the lengthening of *Qui pridie quam pateretur* to *Qui pridie
quam pro nostra omniumque salute . . .* ("Who the night before
He suffered to save us and all men"), which we use only on
Maundy Thursday. The words *mysterium fidei* ("the mystery
of faith"), during the words of consecration of the chalice, are
a theological explanatory phrase which has never been satis-
factorily accounted for. The phrase occurs in 1 Tim. iii. 9, but
there it refers to Christian doctrine and not to the Eucharist.
Here the word *mysterium* almost certainly means "central
sacramental rite" and not "central mystery" in the more
modern sense of a revealed truth which is beyond our full
understanding.

The fact that Our Lord "lifted up His eyes to heaven" is a
detail not recorded in the New Testament accounts. We know,

[1] There is, of course, every reason to think that an account of this part
of the Last Supper was in use among the Christians at their liturgy before
the New Testament accounts were written down or widely known, and that
the account given by St. Luke and St. Paul reflects that already in use in the
liturgy.

Qui pridie . . . elevatis oculis . . .

. . . benedixit . . .

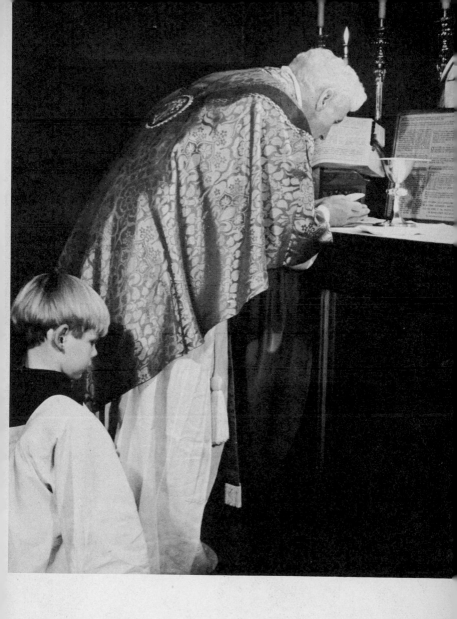

Hoc est enim Corpus meum

Elevation of the Host

43

Hic est enim calix Sanguinis mei . . .

Elevation of the chalice

however, from accounts of Jewish ritual that He would have grasped the cup with both hands (as the priest does at this point) and raised it up slightly as a gesture of offering to God, so He would quite naturally have raised His eyes at the same time. The priest's gestures during this Consecration follow the words, in an attempt to do exactly what Our Lord did. The Elevation of the Host grew up at the end of the eleventh century out of the gesture of raising up the host (and then the chalice) slightly at the words *accepit panem* ("took bread"), which occur before its consecration. People wanted to see the Host *after* its consecration, and so the elevation began, with the result that the gesture of raising the host slightly at *accepit* fell into disuse. The elevation of the chalice came later, with the devotion to the Blessed Sacrament of the fourteenth century, as the congregation only see the chalice itself and not the consecrated Wine, and this elevation does not appear in the Roman missal till the sixteenth century.[1]

We first learn of the ringing of the bell about A.D. 1200 as a call to adoration before the elevation rather than accompanying it, just as it is still rung in some countries before the (much older) Little Elevation. The faithful, referred to in the *Memento* for the Living as "*standing* round", began to go down on their knees when the practice of elevating the Host began; the custom spread of them all kneeling till the Communion, and finally from the beginning of the Canon till the Communion. The kneeling came to be given more importance than the looking up at the Host (for which the elevation had been introduced) and the faithful often bow their heads down during the elevation. When everyone was *already* kneeling on both knees, priests began to feel that *they* should make some reverence at this point, so, at first only bowing, they eventually genuflected— on one knee, because holding the Host or chalice. By this very

---

[1] It is owing to this late insertion of an elevation of the chalice that the slight raising of the chalice (at *accipiens . . . calicem*) did *not* fall into disuse.

devious route the practice of genuflection on one knee first entered the Roman rite in the fourteenth century. It had long been customary as a reverence to temporal lords, but had hitherto had no place in liturgy, and still has none in Eastern liturgy. From this place in the Mass its other uses developed; now the priest genuflects every time he touches either Host or chalice between the Consecration and Communion, both before and after doing so.

During the elevation the server lifted the hem of the celebrant's vestment to free his arms for the elevation in the days of more copious vestments. This gesture had belonged to the deacon long before there was any question of genuflecting, so it has nothing to do with assisting the priest's genuflection.

Unde et memores, Domine, nos servi tui, sed et plebs tua sancta, ejusdem Christi Filii tui Domini nostri tam beatae passionis, nec non et ab inferis resurrectionis, sed et in coelos gloriosae ascensionis: offerimus praeclarae majestati tuae de tuis donis, ac datis, hostiam puram, hostiam sanctam, hostiam immaculatam, Panem sanctum vitae aeternae, et Calicem salutis perpetuae.

Wherefore, O Lord, we Thy servants, as also Thy holy people, calling to mind the blessed passion of the same Christ Thy Son our Lord, His resurrection from the dead, and admirable ascension into heaven, offer unto Thy most excellent Majesty, of Thy gifts bestowed upon us, a pure Host, a holy Host, an unspotted Host, the holy Bread of eternal life, and Chalice of everlasting salvation.

Unde et memores. The prayers that immediately follow the Consecration have the character of drawing out the meaning of what has been done already in the *Qui pridie*, of making more explicit what is there implicit; thus the Eastern rites follow the institution-narrative by an invocation of the power of the Holy Spirit on the Bread and Wine, which also occurs at this place in the earliest text we have of the Roman Canon. In our present Mass this idea comes in before the Consecration, in the prayer for consecration (*Quam oblationem*) and during the Offertory (*Veni sanctificator*).

Two ideas now come particularly to the fore, recollection of Our Lord and offering: "Wherefore, calling to mind . . .

we offer" (*Unde et memores . . . offerimus*). St. Paul immediately follows his account of Our Lord's institution of the Eucharist by saying: "So it is the Lord's death you are heralding, whenever you eat this bread and drink this cup, until He comes" (1 Cor. xi. 26).[1] So we, too, immediately after the Consecration, call to mind Our Lord's death, His sacrifice: "calling to mind the blessed passion of the same Christ, Thy Son, our Lord, and also His resurrection from the dead and His admirable ascension into heaven, do offer . . ."—we make *our* sacrifice. All this sequence of thought, and the precise wording *memores . . . offerimus*, is already present in the Roman Canon in the earliest known text of it, from the third century. This third century Canon calls to mind the Death and Resurrection, and the Ascension is already included by the fourth century—the three together forming parts of the one sacrifice of Christ, its consummation on Calvary and its acceptance by the Father. "We offer" is the main verb, so this is the central sacrificial prayer of the Mass among those which make explicit the meaning of the sacrifice consummated by the *Qui pridie*. The "we" who offer comprises the celebrant and assisting clergy ("thy servants") and the whole congregation present ("thy holy people"). We offer "of thine own gifts", unlike the offerings in pagan sacrifices, "a clean victim, a holy victim, a spotless victim": these latter phrases, too, consciously point the difference between this and all other sacrifices.

Supra quae propitio ac sereno vultu respicere digneris: et accepta habere, sicuti accepta habere dignatus es munera pueri tui justi Abel, et sacrificium Patriarchae nostri Abrahae: et quod tibi obtulit summus sacerdos tuus Melchisedech, sanctum sacrificium, immaculatam hostiam.

Upon which vouchsafe to look with a propitious and serene countenance, and to accept them, as Thou wast graciously pleased to accept the gifts of Thy just servant Abel, and the sacrifice of our patriarch Abraham, and that which Thy high priest, Melchisedech, offered to Thee, a holy sacrifice and unspotted victim.

[1] We must again remember that the Eucharist was already being celebrated when St. Paul wrote, and that his words may well be guided by the words customary in the Eucharist.

Supplices te rogamus, omnipotens Deus: jube haec perferri per manus sancti Angeli tui in sublime altare tuum, in conspectu divinae majestatis tuae: ut quotquot ex hac altaris participatione sacrosanctum Filii tui Corpus et Sanguinem sumpserimus, omni benedictione coelesti et gratia repleamur. Per eumdem Christum Dominum nostrum. Amen.

We most humbly beseech Thee, almighty God, to command that these sacrifices be borne in the hands of Thy holy angel to Thine altar on high, before the sight of Thy divine majesty, that so many as are partakers of the precious Body and Blood of Thy Son at this altar may be filled with all heavenly benediction and grace. Through the same Christ our Lord. Amen.

Supra quae and **Supplices.** These two prayers will be taken together because both continue and develop the idea of offering introduced by *Unde et memores*, and because they seem to have occurred at first in the opposite order. They both ask God to accept our offering.

The *Supra quae* recognises that we can only *proffer*: God must accept; and even though our Victim is supremely acceptable and for ever accepted, we are offering ourselves with Him, and so pray God to look kindly on our offering. It is to the outward appearance that the prayer immediately refers (the bread and the chalice of the previous prayer) and we ourselves provided that outward appearance and are symbolised by it. Just as the previous prayer consciously distinguishes our sacrifice from all pagan sacrifices, so this one consciously links it to the great sacrifices of the Old Testament; it serves to remind us that, though the Victim we offer is incomparably greater, yet the victim is not the whole of sacrifice—we, too, must have the inward sacrificial dispositions, the surrender to God, which these great Old Testament figures brought to their self-offering. Abel offered a lamb, Abraham his son; we offer the Lamb of God who is the Son of God. Melchisedech (cf. Gen. xiv. 18) is taken as a type of the priesthood of Christ in the Epistle to the Hebrews, chapters v. and vii. There the thought primarily is that Melchisedech is like Christ in that he stands alone; he is not one of a line of similar priests, as were the Jewish priests, and in that sense Christ is a priest " of the order of Melchisedech,

Supplices te rogamus . . .

Memento for the dead

a priest for ever" (Ps. cix. 4). The thought that Melchisedech offered bread and wine is secondary, but his offering, like ours, is here declared to be a holy and spotless one probably in defiance of those heretics who considered all matter to be evil and the Eucharistic offering to be therefore an unspiritual one.[1]

In the *Supplices* ("We most humbly beseech . . .") we ask that our offering may not only be looked on favourably but carried up to God. In asking that the angel(s) should perform this office, the prayer carries on the thought of the Preface which associates the angelic worship with ours. The idea that "the Angel" here is Christ, the "Angel of great Counsel",[2] is an interpretation which first appears in the twelfth century,[3] reminding us that Christ is Priest in this sacrifice, as He is Victim, and that our priesthood is a share in His, even as only in Him can we hope to be victims acceptable and fit to be offered to God. Mention occurs in the Apocalypse (viii. 3–4) of "the golden altar which is before the throne of God", and of the angel whose duty it is there to offer the prayers of the Church; the imagery brings out the idea that our altar is in a sense transported to heaven and becomes an altar before the very throne of God, when Christ is the Victim laid upon it. Half-way through the *Supplices* the thought moves from Consecration to Communion, from sacrifice to sacrament; we pray that God may receive our offering in such a way that all of us who partake of it[4] (communicate) "may be filled with every

---

[1] One curious mistranslation occurs here: in Genesis Melchisedech is called " priest of the most high God "; here he has become " high priest (of God) ".

[2] So the Old Roman version of the Old Testament translates Isa. ix. 6 in the Introit for the third Mass of Christmas Day—*magni consilii angelus*.

[3] The earliest text of the Roman Canon in which this thought appears (fourth century) has *per manus angelorum tuorum*, speaking of " angels " in the plural.

[4] Note that the Latin says: " by this sharing in the altar "; and not: " by the sharing in this altar ". So, *ex hac altaris participatione* means that we have a share in the heavenly altar, just mentioned, on which our Gift is now presumed to lie. The Consecration effected at Mass gives us a share in the one eternal sacrifice of Christ, lying for ever on the " heavenly altar ".

heavenly blessing and grace". The prayer is one for the acceptance of our sacrifice and *therefore* for the fruitful reception of Communion. It therefore presupposes: (1) that all are going to receive Communion; (2) that only by receiving Communion do we have our full share in the sacrifice. "By receiving Holy Communion the faithful take part in the Sacrifice."[1]

The priest's deep bow during the first half of the *Supplices*, as in the *Te igitur*, is a very old gesture of suppliant offering; he kisses the altar as he says "are partakers . . . at this altar"; the crosses over Host and chalice are gestures of indicating, as in the *Te igitur*; the signing of himself at "every . . . blessing" comes from the late Middle Ages. As in the *Communicantes*, the phrase *Per Christum Dominum nostrum* is a repetition of the theme introduced by the Preface and not really a closing formula, the *Amen* being a late addition.

Memento etiam, Domine, famulorum, famularumque tuarum N. et N., qui nos praecesserunt cum signo fidei, et dormiunt in somno pacis.	Remember also, O Lord, Thy servants, N. and N., who are gone hence before us with the sign of faith, and sleep the sleep of peace.

(A pause)

Ipsis, Domine, et omnibus in Christo quiescentibus locum refrigerii, lucis et pacis, ut indulgeas, deprecamur. Per eundem Christum Dominum nostrum. Amen.	To these, O Lord, and to all who sleep in Christ, we pray Thee grant a place of refreshment, light and peace. Through the same Christ our Lord. Amen.

Memento etiam and **Ipsis Domine.** These formulas together form the Commemoration of the Dead, and with the next prayer, *Nobis quoque*, make up a second block of Intercessory Prayers inserted into the Canon, balancing the block from *Te igitur* to *Hanc igitur* inserted before the Consecration.[2] The practice of making some mention of the dead in the Mass is heard of in the third century—but not at this place. They

---

[1] Pius XII, Encyclical *Mediator Dei*, English trans. § 126; see also § 122: "The Communion belongs to the integration of the Sacrifice."
[2] See p. 115.

would probably have had a place in the old Intercessory Prayers
after the Synaxis, and have continued for a time, when the
Eucharist and Synaxis had been joined, to receive some mention
during the Offertory, before all the ideas of the Intercessory
Prayers had been transferred to the Canon. Then, too, one of
the earlier forms of the *Hanc igitur*, which we have seen to have
been a variable formula for expressing the intentions for which
the Mass is being offered, is arranged as a commemoration of
the dead. But the idea of *naming* the dead persons is later than
that of naming the living; at any rate from the eighth century,
the deacon would read out the names of the particular dead for
whom the Mass was being offered after ". . . in the sleep of
peace", and before the priest went on, "To these . . ." For a
long time this *Memento* for the dead was only said at Masses
which were being specially offered for the dead (*Requiem*
Masses), or was omitted on Sundays[1] and big feasts, and in a
few places this practice lasted till the fourteenth century.

The opening words, *Memento etiam* ("Remember also"),
have suggested to some that this Commemoration once came
immediately after the first *Memento*, for the living, but it is
just as satisfactory to take the "also" as following from the
previous prayer; we have prayed that the full benefits of our
Eucharist may be granted to us, so now we pray that the dead
also may share in these graces. The thought has moved towards
Communion, and so we naturally think of the one family of the
Church that shares together in the table of the Lord and the
altar of His sacrifice. The "sign of faith" (*signum fidei*) is the
character impressed by Baptism: only Christians are mentioned
in the Eucharistic Prayer, and our dead fellow-Christians stand
before God marked indelibly with this sign of faith as members
of the one family, claiming, as it were, their share in the graces
of the Eucharist. The Commemoration is full of reminiscences:

[1] A seventh-century source tells us that the Commemoration for the dead
was omitted on Sundays because Our Lord Himself gives rest to those who
die on His own (the Lord's) day.

refrigerium (refreshment) and *praecessit in pace*, "(s)he has gone before us in peace", and similar formulas are found on Christian tombs, the "peace" being thought of both as the peace of (unity with) the Church and as the happiness of heaven;[1] St. Paul speaks of death as a sleep, as Our Lord had done (Matt. ix. 24 and John xi. 11), and of those who have slept through Jesus, the dead who are in Christ (1 Thess. iv. 13–17; cf. Apoc. xiv. 13). The *Per Christum Dominum nostrum* is, again, the repetition of a theme rather than a closing formula. It is quite unique in liturgy that the priest should bow his head at this formula as he does here, and various explanations have been given; some think the bow really belongs to the word *deprecamur* ("we beseech thee"); and it has often been connected with the fact that Our Lord bowed His head when He died, an appropriate reminiscence in this prayer for the dead.

Nobis quoque peccatoribus famulis tuis, de multitudine miserationum tuarum sperantibus, partem aliquam, et societatem donare digneris, cum tuis sanctis Apostolis et Martyribus: cum Joanne, Stephano, Matthia, Barnaba, Ignatio, Alexandro, Marcellino, Petro, Felicitate, Perpetua, Agatha, Lucia, Agnete, Caecilia, Anastasia, et omnibus Sanctis tuis: intra quorum nos consortium, non aestimator meriti, sed veniae, quaesumus, largitor, admitte. Per Christum Dominum nostrum.

Also to us sinners Thy servants, confiding in the multitude of Thy mercies, vouchsafe to grant some part and fellowship with Thy holy apostles and Martyrs; with John, Stephen, Matthias, Barnabas, Ignatius, Alexander, Marcellinus, Peter, Felicity, Perpetua, Agatha, Lucy, Agnes, Cecily, Anastasia, and with all Thy saints; into whose company we beseech Thee to admit us, not in consideration of our merit, but of Thine own gratuitous pardon. Through Christ our Lord.

Nobis quoque peccatoribus. This is one of the latest prayers to enter the Canon in its present developed form. It remains uncertain whether, when first introduced, it was always said or only when the Commemoration for the dead was made; and therefore whether *quoque* ("also") takes up from *Memento* or *Supplices*. The oldest layer in the prayer seems to be the transition to the idea of eternal life, fellowship with the saints;

---

[1] The two ideas are not wholly distinct.

we asked at the end of the *Supplices* to be filled with every heavenly grace, and here, with the idea of Communion more prominent, we ask for eternal life as a fellowship with the saints: this repetition of the notion of the Communion of Saints leads to a further list of them being mentioned. The prayer, then, repeats after the Consecration the theme the *Communicantes* had introduced before it; there we wished to be joined to the saints in offering the sacrifice, here we ask to be joined in closer union with them in the coming sacrament.

Though the ideas which this prayer introduces are common to and belong to all of us, it is, as it stands, a prayer for the clergy. The voice of the priest is slightly, not fully, raised at the first three words—an indication that he is notifying the assisting clergy of something (cf. the *Orate fratres*); this was the moment when the subdeacons, who had been bowing since the beginning of the Preface, stood erect. Then, the very humble tone of the prayer, both at the beginning and end, shows that by "we sinners" is meant the celebrant and his assistants who, conscious of the awful dignity of their office, pray that they, too, may share in the heavenly grace which at the end of the *Supplices* they begged from God in the name of all. Again at the end of the prayer the refrain occurs, *Per Christum Dominum nostrum*; no *Amen* could be added here as the next prayer ("Through whom . . .") follows straight on.

The names in this prayer are, like those in the *Communicantes*, very carefully arranged. They reflect the devotion to special saints that had grown up at Rome in the fifth and sixth centuries; Gregory I, we know, added Agatha and Lucy and probably remodelled this prayer in other ways. We have here John the Baptist followed by fourteen martyrs, seven men and seven women. Stephen (a deacon) comes first as being the first Christian martyr, and then the men are arranged hierarchically: Matthias took Judas's place among the apostles and Barnabas, the fellow-worker of Paul, is called an apostle in

Acts xiv. 13. Ignatius was bishop of Antioch; Alexander is called both bishop and priest in different versions of his story; Marcellinus was a priest and Peter an exorcist. The women show a certain geographical arrangement, Perpetua coming from Africa, Agatha and Lucy from Sicily, Agnes and Cecily from Rome and Anastasia from the East (Sirmium); Felicity, who comes first, is certainly the Roman martyr of that name and not Perpetua's slave Felicity (who is mentioned in all lists *after* Perpetua), but it is just possible that whoever finally gave the list its present form confused the two.

Per quem haec omnia, Domine, semper bona creas, sanctificas, vivificas, benedicis, et praestas nobis.

By whom, O Lord, Thou ever dost create, sanctify, quicken, bless and bestow upon us all these good things.

Per ipsum, et cum ipso, et in ipso, est tibi Deo Patri omnipotenti, in unitate Spiritus sancti, omnis honor et gloria,

By Him, and with Him, and in Him, is unto Thee, God the Father almighty, in the unity of the Holy Ghost all honour and glory,

(*aloud*)

per omnia saecula saeculorum.
M. Amen.

for ever and ever.
S. Amen.

Per quem haec omnia. Both this and the next prayer, *Per ipsum*, have the ring of conclusions (summing up the whole Eucharistic Prayer), though the latter is the doxology proper. The first formula, *Per quem*, we know to have been in use for the blessing of various objects such as milk, honey, etc., and the bishop still blesses the oils at this place on Maundy Thursday. The custom of introducing such a blessing-formula into the Canon was due to people wanting to have the blessings linked as closely as possible with the Blessing, the Eucharistic Prayer. We have already noted that many other gifts apart from those of bread and wine were brought up in the Offertory procession, and these would be placed beside the altar; well into the Middle Ages many natural objects were blessed at this point, apart from those given to the Church. This fact accounts for the

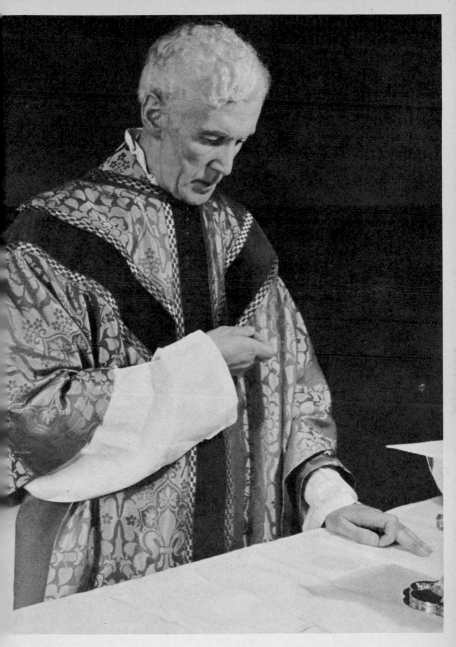

Nobis quoque peccatoribus . . .

Per ipsum . . . est tibi Deo Patri

wording of the prayer[1] which does not primarily refer to the Bread and Wine now already consecrated, though these are included as may be seen from the last phrase, *praestas nobis* ("dost give to us"), which has the coming Communion in mind. The prayer is not a petition for a blessing, but a recognition and appreciation of the great Blessing, the Consecration, that has already taken place. The petition of the *Te igitur*, "that thou wouldst vouchsafe to accept and bless these gifts", has been answered.

Per Ipsum ("By Him . . . all honour and glory.") All formal prayer of the Church concludes with doxology, statement of God's existing glory—the psalms of the Office, the Collect, Secret and Post-Communion. Here is the greatest doxology in the liturgy, concluding the Prayer of the Church. Its very wording goes back to our oldest text of the Roman Canon in the third century, and already in the earliest days of Christianity St. Paul concluded most of his written prayers with a doxology.

During the *Per quem* the priest makes three Signs of the Cross with his hand at the words *sanctificas, vivificas, benedicis* ("sanctify, quicken, bless"), the accompanying of such words with this gesture being a medieval practice. During the *Per Ipsum* he makes five more crosses: three with the Host over the chalice, at the words *ipsum . . . ipso . . . ipso*; two more with the Host between the lip of the chalice and his own breast, at the words *Deo Patri* and *Spiritus sancti* ("God the Father . . . Holy Ghost"). The growth of such blessings during the Middle Ages, particularly in Gallican lands, was accompanied by great diversity both of practice and of symbolic meaning attached to the practice: the five were taken as

[1] A great deal of theology is packed into these few words: against those who declare matter evil it is roundly asserted that God made His creation good, as Genesis says; here, too, we find the doctrine that God created through the Word—*per ipsum . . . creas*; and the exchange of gifts between God and man is suggested.

representing the wounds of Christ, whose death is here shown forth, the gesture at the side of (not over) the chalice representing the wound in the side of Christ;[1] or the two larger crosses (sometimes four were made) at the side of the chalice were taken to mean that Christ was extended, in the Church, to the four winds, in fulfilment of His own prophecy that when cruci-fied He would draw all things to Himself (John xii. 32).

But all these medieval blessings and interpretations were overlaid upon, and to some extent obscured, the much older gesture which came in this place and which clearly designated that this was the climax of the Eucharistic Prayer; the bringing of the Host to the side of the chalice was itself an older ritual than any of these explanations of it, as we shall see.

In the solemn liturgy of Rome, as it is described for us in the seventh century, the archdeacon *raised aloft* the chalice from *Per Ipsum* right down to the people's *Amen*, i.e. all through the doxology. The Pope at the same time raised the Host, touching the side of the elevated chalice with It—to signify the unity of the two elements in one sacrament. This was the elevation, now called the Little Elevation, which was customary at least five hundred years before our present elevation at the Consecration. It was never connected with the people seeing the Host, but was always a gesture of offering to God to accompany the great doxology. The introduction first of three and then of two more blessings at the beginning of the doxology caused the elevation to be confined to the last few words, but till the fifteenth century it was still done through the final *Per omnia saecula saeculorum, Amen*, which was said aloud. Then, however, the introduction of the rule of genuflections (before and after touching Host and/or chalice), caused a break just before the *Per omnia* for the priest's genuflection, so that now he raises Host and chalice together only while saying *omnis honor et*

---

[1] It is a very ancient Christian idea that the Church sprang from the side of Christ as He lay dead on the Cross, as Eve from the side of Adam during his sleep.

. . . *per omnia saecula saeculorum.   Amen.*

Pater noster . . .

gloria ("all honour and glory"). One cannot escape the impression that the later practices—the silent Canon, the blessings, the genuflections—have broken up the great doxology and robbed it of its sense of climax. When the priest says *Per omnia saecula saeculorum* aloud, with the Host replaced on the corporal, the chalice covered and the genuflection made, he seems to be beginning something new.

The *Per Ipsum*, the great doxology, is the final and triumphant elaboration of the theme of "through Christ Our Lord" which the Eucharistic Prayer introduces in its opening phrases in the Preface and constantly resumes throughout. From the earliest times the whole people assembled finally answered the last pronouncement of the theme with their great act of assent, *Amen*.

THE BREAKING AND COMMUNION

Oremus.
Praeceptis salutaribus moniti, et divina institutione formati, audemus dicere.
Pater noster, qui es in coelis: sanctificetur nomen tuum: adveniat regnum tuum: fiat voluntas tua, sicut in coelo, et in terra: panem nostrum quotidianum da nobis hodie: et dimitte nobis debita nostra, sicut et nos dimittimus debitoribus nostris; et ne nos inducas in tentationem.
M. Sed libera nos a malo.
S. Amen.

Let us pray.
Instructed by Thy saving precepts, and following Thy divine instructions, we presume to say:
Our Father, who art in heaven, hallowed be Thy name; Thy kingdom come; Thy will be done on earth as it is in heaven; give us this day our daily bread; and forgive us our trespasses, as we forgive them that trespass against us; and lead us not into temptation.
S. But deliver us from evil.
P. Amen.

Oremus . . . Pater Noster. Gregory I put the *Pater* in this place,[1] because he considered that it should be said over the Body of Christ, and not when the Bread had already been removed from the altar to the side, where the Breaking then took place. Now, of course, both Host and chalice remain on the altar all the time till the Communion.

[1] There is no certain evidence that the *Pater* came elsewhere in the Roman Mass before his time, but comparison with practice elsewhere in the West makes it highly probable.

The first three petitions of the Our Father sum up the leading ideas of the Eucharistic Prayer—the praise and glory given to God in this sacrifice of His Son—and from "Give us this day our daily bread" onwards we look forward to Holy Communion and its effects, and ask for forgiveness of our sins before we approach the Sacrament. It is very likely that the faithful said the Our Father at the reception of Holy Communion even before it was formally introduced into the Mass—for example, when they gave themselves Holy Communion at home during the week; it occurs everywhere in the early rites for Communion to the sick. The Our Father came under the short-lived law of secrecy[1] and was among the things Christians were not allowed to divulge to pagans: this may account for the terms of awe of the introductory prayer ("we make bold—we dare— to say"), though even apart from this Our Lord's own prayer would naturally be approached with special reverence. In the East the Pater was said (or sung) by everyone, but Gregory tells us that at Rome it was by the priest alone, though everyone came in with the last petition, "But deliver us from evil". This question is mixed up with that of the melodies for singing it, of which the more complicated ones seem to be the older and so would be left to the clergy. It is worth noting here that we still say aloud at Low Mass, and sing at High Mass, the parts of the Canon and Communion for which special melodies were written (the whole Eucharistic Prayer being at one time chanted aloud by the priest in a simple tone)—viz. *Sanctus, Benedictus, Pater* and *Agnus Dei*, and of course the Communion chant, though this was for long not said by the priest at all.

The addition of *Amen* to the *Pater* first appears in the ninth century, being taken over from the established Latin text of the Bible (the Vulgate). It breaks the unity of the episode, in which "deliver us from evil", said by everyone, is continued by the priest's "Deliver us, we beseech Thee. . . " (the *Libera*),

---

[1] See p. 35.

Wiping the paten before the Libera

Kissing the paten

and was never said by the people: it is added on quietly by the priest after this response.[1]

Libera nos, quaesumus, Domine, ab omnibus malis, praeteritis, praesentibus, et futuris: et intercedente beata et gloriosa semper Virgine Dei Genetrice Maria, cum beatis Apostolis tuis Petro et Paulo, atque Andrea, et omnibus Sanctis, da propitius pacem in diebus nostris: ut ope misericordiae tuae adjuti, et a peccato simus semper liberi, et ab omni perturbatione securi.

Deliver us, we beseech Thee, O Lord, from all evils, past, present, and to come; and by the intercession of the blessed and glorious Mary, ever Virgin Mother of God, and of the holy Apostles Peter and Paul, and Andrew and of all the saints, mercifully grant peace in our days, that through the assistance of Thy mercy we may be always free from sin, and secure from all disturbance.

Per eumdem Dominum nostrum Jesum Christum Filium tuum:

Through Jesus Christ, Thy Son, our Lord:

Here he breaks the Host

Qui tecum vivit et regnat in unitate Spiritus sancti Deus.

Who liveth and reigneth with Thee in the unity of the Holy Ghost.

aloud

Per omnia saecula saeculorum.
M. Amen.

For ever and ever.
S. Amen.

With the fragment he then makes the sign of the Cross thrice over the chalice, saying

S. Pax Domini sit semper vobiscum.
M. Et cum spiritu tuo.

P. The peace of the Lord be always with you.
S. And with thy spirit.

Then he puts the fragment into the chalice, saying

Haec commixtio, et consecratio Corporis et Sanguinis Domini nostri Jesu Christi, fiat accipientibus nobis in vitam aeternam. Amen.

May this mingling and consecrating of the Body and Blood of Our Lord Jesus Christ avail us that receive it unto life everlasting. Amen.

Libera. Pax. Haec commixtio. A good deal has already been said about these prayers and about the way in which all that is left in our Mass of the Breaking and Mingling now occurs while they are being said. Most rites show an elaboration of the concluding words of the *Pater* at this point, the insistence on our deliverance from sin being due to St. Paul's warnings about receiving Communion unworthily (1 Cor. xi. 27, etc.); that sin is chiefly envisaged in this mention of evil is shown by the fact that we ask to be delivered from past evils. Till

[1] The *silent* Amen is a twentieth-century rubric, the *Ritus servandus* having *submissa voce*.

about 900 the *Libera* was continued, after the more intricate singing of the *Pater*, in the simple tone used for the whole Canon, and is still said aloud on Good Friday. This part of the Good Friday liturgy is a Communion service and therefore begins with the *Pater* and its introduction;[1] it was usual for everyone to receive Holy Communion on Good Friday till about the end of the fifteenth century. The continued saying aloud of the *Libera* on Good Friday is due to the fact that from about A.D. 800 this part of the Mass was taken to represent the Passion, the "breaking" of Our Lord's Body, the symbolism ending with the Mingling which represented the return of life to Our Lord's Body at the Resurrection.[2]

During the concluding formula, *Per eumdem Dominum* ("Through the same Jesus Christ . . ."), the priest breaks the Host into three pieces,[3] i.e. he first breaks It in half and then breaks a small portion off the left half, placing the portion in the chalice after he has said *Pax Domini* ("The peace of the Lord . . ."). The introduction into the *Libera* of all that is left in our Mass of the Breaking seems to be due to two factors. (1) At a priest's (not at a bishop's) Mass the *fermentum*[4] was placed in the chalice at *Pax Domini*; if a portion is now to be placed in the chalice at this point, the priest must previously break his own Host. The *fermentum* was closely connected with the Kiss of Peace because both signify the unity and harmony of the Church, and so was placed in the chalice at the words

[1] The previous saying of *In spiritu humilitatis* and *Orate fratres* (to which no answer is given) comes in with the prayers at the incensing of the *oblata* and is a late addition—and a very extraordinary one, seeing that no sacrifice is offered: but it is worthy of note that the priest first washes his hands without saying the *Lavabo*—another old survival.

[2] These ideas appear in the East as early as the sixth century.

[3] These pieces were laid on the altar at the Pope's Mass, one for the *fermentum*, one for Communion to the sick and one for his own Communion. The medieval symbolism of the Threefold Body of Christ (on earth, in heaven, in the Church) caused the breaking into three to continue at a time when, with the introduction of small hosts, a breaking into two parts would have been sufficient for a piece to be placed in the chalice.

[4] See p. 45.

The Breaking: . . . *per eundem Dominum nostrum* . . .

Pax Domini . . .

Pax Domini, which are the signal for the faithful to give the Kiss of Peace; our ritual derives from that of the priest (who would be receiving the *fermentum*) and not of the bishop (who would be sending it). (2) To all this is added the symbolism of the Passion (breaking) and Resurrection (mingling). "Peace be with you" was Our Lord's Easter greeting; this is a further factor in the introduction of the breaking into the *Libera*, for the breaking must precede the mingling in order that there may be a piece of the Host to place in the chalice. There was some tendency in the Middle Ages to put the prayer which accompanies the actual mingling, *Haec commixtio* ("May this mingling . . ."), before the *Pax Domini*, because the Resurrection (symbolised by mingling) actually took place before the Easter greeting (*Pax*); but the established practice of three crosses made with the portion of the Host over the chalice at *Pax Domini* overrode this tendency. These crosses go back to the eighth century and belong to the symbolism of Our Lord's death on the Cross: at first only one cross was made; the extension to three may be part of the general tendency to multiply these blessings, or may have been meant to represent the three days during which Our Lord was dead.

The paten was originally used at the Breaking—which did not take place at the altar. It was brought to the celebrant during the *Libera*, and still is at High Mass: at Low Mass the priest removes it during the *Libera* from under the corporal where it has lain since the Offertory, signs himself with it, kisses it before slipping it under the Host and then breaks the Host. We get some idea of the original size of the paten from the detailed description of the Pope's Mass in the seventh century, in which we are told that it was held in front of him by two kneeling subdeacons, as he sat at his throne, so that he could break the Bread over it. In the late Middle Ages the rule for its size still was that its diameter should be the same as the height of the chalice. That the paten should be brought to the altar at all was a result of the dwindling of the full rite of breaking, and the latest development of all is its being carried in from the beginning on top of the chalice, with a consequent shrinking of its size to one which fits it to rest conveniently there. Till well into the Middle Ages the Host was still broken over the paten; now It is broken over the chalice, but the two halves are laid on the paten, which is also used at the Ablutions for collecting any fragments of the Host that may remain on the corporal. When the deacon began bringing up the paten to the altar, he kissed it before handing it to the priest, as a sign of reverence for the sacred vessel on which the broken Host was to lie;[1] then later the priest kissed it; since the twelfth century he signs himself with it and kisses it afterwards.

Agnus Dei, qui tollis peccata mundi: miserere nobis. (*twice*)

Agnus Dei, qui tollis peccata mundi: dona nobis pacem.

Domine Jesu Christe, qui dixisti Apostolis tuis: Pacem relinquo vobis, pacem meam do vobis: ne respicias peccata mea, sed fidem Ecclesiae tuae; eamque secundum voluntatem tuam pacificare et coadunare digneris: Qui vivis et regnas Deus per omnia saecula saeculorum. Amen.

Lamb of God, who takest away the sins of the world: have mercy on us. (*twice*)

Lamb of God, who takest away the sins of the world: give us peace.

O Lord Jesus Christ, who didst say to Thy apostles, Peace I leave you, My peace I give unto you; look not upon my sins but upon the faith of Thy Church; and vouchsafe to grant her peace and union according to Thy will: who livest and reignest God for ever and ever. Amen.

Agnus Dei.   As this chant belongs to the breaking it does not occur on Good Friday, when the breaking for Communion would have been done the day before. This chant by the people, imported into Rome in the late seventh century probably by Eastern priests in flight from Islam, was not said by the priest; we first hear of this practice in the eleventh century and do not

[1] Various early medieval instructions show how the paten should be held by an acolyte with a linen cloth till wanted. The posture of the subdeacon during High Mass, who holds it in the humeral veil from the Offertory to the *Libera*, seems an exaggerated version of this, but may also be connected with the rather obscure rite of the *sancta* (see p. 45), which would have lain on the paten from the beginning of Mass, though at that time the paten was too large and heavy for a subdeacon to hold it for so long by himself.

Agnus Dei . . .

The priest's prayers before Communion

know how long it had already been customary, but by this time it had been connected with the Kiss of Peace (*dona nobis pacem*) and no longer with the breaking. The people continued to sing it till the eleventh century, when the melodies became more intricate and it was relegated to the choir. This whole process was a result of the abolition of the breaking in the ninth and tenth centuries. At first repeated as often as was necessary, during the breaking, the *Agnus Dei* begins to be fixed at three repetitions in the ninth century; in the next two centuries the third acclamation is changed to *dona nobis pacem* and towards the end of the same period the termination *dona eis requiem* (*sempiternam*) ("grant them eternal rest") comes into use at Masses for the dead.

Domini Jesu Christe qui dixisti ("O Lord Jesus Christ, who said . . .") and **Kiss of Peace** (at High Mass). The prayer for peace, the first in the Roman rite to be addressed to Our Lord, though it first appears in Europe in the eleventh century, was still not customary in many places when it was included in Pius V's missal. But this prayer, where customary, and the others connected with the Kiss of Peace (*Pax Domini* and *Agnus Dei*) continued to be said even when the kiss was not given. In the case of *Pax Domini* this was because of the connection it had acquired with the ritual of mingling. Further, all this part of the Mass had come to be regarded as a preparation for Communion, as indeed the Kiss of Peace always had been. With the dwindling of the practice of all receiving Communion, the kiss and the prayers connected with it began to be considered in the tenth century in the light of a spiritual Communion, a substitute for sacramental Communion, though previously only those about to receive Communion had exchanged the *Pax*. The older practice was for a priest to bring the *Pax* from the bishop to the congregation, but this gave way to the people simply turning and giving it each to his neighbour; the segregation of the sexes in church would eliminate any embarrassment or distractions. There were different ways of giving the Pax, but eventually any form of embrace was replaced, among the congregation, by the *osculatorium*: this was a picture of Our Lord, a relic, or some similar object passed round the congregation and kissed by each in turn; this practice originated in England in the thirteenth century—and very English it is, too! Since the end of the thirteenth century the *Pax* has only been given at High Mass, and then only among persons of some liturgical standing; it is still given throughout cathedral chapters and monastic choirs. The connection of the *Agnus Dei* with the idea of peace and the insertion of a prayer for peace has caused the Kiss to be separated from the *Pax Domini*. As explained earlier, before the fifth century, as still in the Eastern rites, the *Pax* came at the beginning of the Offertory.

Domine Jesu Christe, Fili Dei vivi, qui ex voluntate Patris, co-operante Spiritu sancto, per mortem tuam mundum vivificasti: libera me per hoc sacrosanctum Corpus et Sanguinem tuum ab omnibus iniquitatibus meis, et universis malis: et fac me tuis semper inhaerere mandatis, et a te numquam separari permittas: qui cum eodem Deo Patre, et Spiritu sancto vivis et regnas Deus in saecula saeculorum. Amen.

Lord Jesus Christ, Son of the Living God, who, according to the will of Thy Father, hast by Thy death, through the co-operation of the Holy Ghost, given life to the world; deliver me by this Thy most sacred Body and Blood from all my iniquities, and from all evils, and make me always adhere to Thy commandments, and never suffer me to be separated from Thee, who with the same God the Father and the Holy Ghost livest and reignest God for ever and ever. Amen.

Perceptio Corporis tui, Domine Jesu Christe, quod ego indignus sumere praesumo, non mihi proveniat in judicium et condemnationem: sed pro tua pietate prosit mihi ad tutamentum mentis et corporis, et ad medelam percipiendam: qui vivis et regnas cum Deo Patre in unitate Spiritus sancti Deus, per omnia saecula saeculorum. Amen.

Let not the receiving of Thy Body, O Lord Jesus Christ, which I, all unworthy, presume to take, turn to my judgment and condemnation; but through Thy goodness may it avail me as a safeguard and healing remedy for soul and body: who livest and reignest with God the Father, in the unity of the Holy Ghost, God for ever and ever. Amen.

Panem coelestem accipiam, et nomen Domini invocabo.

I will take the bread of heaven, and call upon the name of the Lord.

Domine non sum dignus . . .

Corpus Domini . . .

Quid retribuam . . .   Collecting the fragments

Receiving the chalice

Domine, non sum dignus, ut intres sub tectum meum: sed tantum dic verbo, et sanabitur anima mea (*thrice*).

Lord, I am not worthy that Thou shouldst enter under my roof; say but the word, and my soul shall be healed.

Receiving both parts of the Host, he says

Corpus Domini nostri Jesu Christi custodiat animam meam in vitam aeternam. Amen.

May the Body of our Lord Jesus Christ preserve my soul to life everlasting. Amen.

Taking the chalice, he says

Quid retribuam Domino pro omnibus quae retribuit mihi? Calicem salutaris accipiam, et nomen Domini invocabo. Laudans invocabo Dominum, et ab inimicis meis salvus ero.

What return shall I make the Lord for all He has given to me? I will take the Chalice of salvation, and call upon the name of the Lord. Praising, I will call upon the Lord, and I shall be saved from my enemies.

Receiving the chalice, he says

Sanguis Domini nostri Jesu Christi custodiat animam meam in vitam aeternam. Amen.

May the blood of our Lord Jesus Christ preserve my soul to everlasting life. Amen.

(*Distribution of Holy Communion*)

Prayers at the Communion. Sufficient has already been said about the prayers of medieval origin which grew up, at first as private devotions, in connection with the Communion of priest and people. We may just observe here that the priest's prayers before consuming the chalice, *Quid retribuam . . . invocabo. Laudans . . .* ("What return shall I make . . . call upon the name of the Lord. Praising I will call . . ."), are from Ps. cxv. 3–4, with the similar expression from Ps. xvii. 4 added on; and that the prayer *Panem coelestem* ("I will take the Bread . . .") was composed as a parallel formula before the reception of the Host. The formulas at the actual reception, *Corpus/Sanguis Domini* ("May the Body/Blood of Our Lord Jesus Christ . . .") actually began as formulas for giving Communion and were later used by the priest at his own reception. They are late formulas, not in use in England, for example, till the fifteenth century.

In the Roman rite of the early centuries Holy Communion was received in one's place in church, the deacon bidding those not communicating to "give place", so that by the sixth century those who were not going to receive Communion may have begun leaving the church after the *Agnus Dei*. Elsewhere the practice of coming up to the altar for Communion is known as early as the fourth century, and also the use of altar rails— breast-high because Holy Communion was received standing till the Middle Ages, when the practice of kneeling spread during the eleventh to sixteenth centuries. In the Stational Mass the Pope brought Holy Communion to all present, followed by the archdeacon with the chalice. Was this Communion under both kinds? We know that the wine brought by the faithful at the Offertory was put in large bowls (*scyphi*) beside the altar, and that only a little of this was drawn off and put into the chalice to be consecrated. There is no reason to think that the wine in the *scyphi* was consecrated, for it did not come to the altar, and the practice of giving the faithful wine into which a particle of the Host had been dipped, or a few drops of the consecrated Wine poured, seems to have been a very early one. The wine in the *scyphi* would be blessed by any general blessing formula (such as the *Per quem*) in the Eucharistic Prayer, but not consecrated; a distinction would be made between the Bread consecrated at the altar and broken for distribution by the celebrant, and this wine.

Quod ore sumpsimus, Domine, pura mente capiamus: et de munere temporali fiat nobis remedium sempiternum.

Grant, O Lord, that what we have taken with our mouth, we may receive with a pure mind, that of a temporal gift it may become to us an eternal remedy.

Corpus tuum, Domine, quod sumpsi, et Sanguis, quem potavi, adhaereat visceribus meis: et praesta: ut in me non remaneat scelerum macula, quem pura et sancta refecerunt sacramenta: qui vivis et regnas in saecula saeculorum. Amen.

May Thy Body, O Lord, which I have received, and Thy Blood which I have drunk, cleave to my bowels; and grant that no stain of sin may remain in me, who have been fed with this pure and holy sacrament: who livest, etc.

People's Communion: *Indulgentiam* . . .

Ecce Agnus Dei . . .

Domine non sum dignus . . .

Corpus Domini . . . custodiat animam tuam . . .

Ablutions and **Reservation.** The two medieval prayers the priest says while performing the ablutions, *Quod ore sumpsimus* and *Corpus tuum Domine*, were both Post-Communions before being used here; the first has been left in the plural, but the second changed to the singular, presumably because its wording suggests that Communion has been received under both kinds—though in fact it is perfectly true to say of all that they have received the Blood of Our Lord. A single concluding formula, *Qui vivis* ("Who livest . . ."), does for both. Many other prayers were used at this place in the Middle Ages and the "Prayer of St. Thomas Aquinas" which occurs in the priest's thanksgiving at the beginning of the missal is a lengthened form of one of them.

The practice of reserving the Blessed Sacrament for the sick (though not at the altar) goes back to the beginning.[1] In the ninth century begins the reservation of the Sacrament in a tabernacle on the altar, though in the thirteenth It was still in many places kept in the sacristy; intermediate usages are those of reservation in a niche in the wall beside or behind the altar, and of suspending the Sacrament above the altar. In the Middle Ages reservation was for the sick, though in the East there were quite a number of weekdays when Communion was given and there was no Mass (and there must have been reservation for the purpose). The faithful always communicated from Hosts consecrated *at that Mass*,[2] Good Friday being quite exceptional in having the "Mass" of the *Pre*sanctified. The present custom of giving Communion from a ciborium kept in the tabernacle has been general only from the sixteenth century. The reception of Communion after Mass is a much

[1] We learn that in the seventh century in the East all that would be required during the ensuing year for Communion to the sick was consecrated on Maundy Thursday: this practice still prevails there, since leavened bread lasts in good condition for much longer than unleavened; it needs to be softened, however, and is dipped into the chalice. In England the custom persevered till the eleventh century.

[2] A practice urged wherever possible by Pius XII in the Encyclical *Mediator Dei* (*Christian Worship*, C.T.S. § 126).

earlier practice, instances being known from the eighth century, though it only became at all general in the twelfth and even led to something like a separation of Communion from the Mass, which the present century has done much to repair.

The rite of Ablutions is first heard of in the East in connection with the purification of the mouth, made necessary by the use of leavened bread. In the West the faithful who had communicated were given a drink of unconsecrated wine long after unleavened bread had come in; the actual rubric[1] ordering this lasted till our own day, but is enforced only at ordinations.

Regulations for the purification of the chalice and the priest's fingers during Mass first occur about A.D. 1000, this previously having been done after Mass; all through the Middle Ages both chalice and fingers were purified at the *piscina*, our present practice (drinking the ablutions) being first mentioned in the thirteenth century as a regulation for a church with no *piscina*. In the eleventh century priests had begun to keep those fingers joined which had touched the *oblata*; they do so now from the elevation of the Host till the ablutions. The combination of the prayers after Communion with the ritual of ablution begins in the thirteenth century.

COMMUNION CHANT

(Ps. cix. 3): In splendoribus sanctorum, ex utero ante luciferum genui te.	In the brightness of the saints, from the womb before the day-star I begot thee.

Communion chant. This is an old chant accompanying the distribution of Communion and is attested even earlier than Introit and Offertory chant. Psalms were used at first, the sign for the *Gloria Patri* being given as the distribution drew to an end, but in the sixth century we find bits of hymns in use and more complex melodies, with the whole chant being sung by the choir instead of the people also having their part. With the lengthening, by embellishment, of the singing of the *Agnus Dei*

[1] See the *Ritus servandus*, XI. 6, at the beginning of the missal.

Ablutions: *Corpus tuum Domine quod sumpsi . . .*

The Communion chant

this latter became the chant sung during the Communion, at least that of the priest. The practice of the priest reading the Communion chant from the missal is attested from the seventh century (as for the Introit), but it is not clear as late as the thirteenth century that he did this when the Mass was being sung. These chants too follow a programme: Ps. i–xxvi for the ferial Masses of Lent (the Thursday Masses of Lent being of later, eighth century, composition, put together from the post-Pentecostal Masses and showing more effort to choose a passage relevant to Communion); Ps. ix–cxviii for the Sundays after Pentecost, though with harvest-time dictating the theme from the eleventh to the fifteenth Sundays and introducing passages from elsewhere in the Bible. The absence of any Communion chant on Good Friday may be a vestige of the earliest centuries before this chant came in, since all could receive Communion on this day till the sixteenth century.

POST-COMMUNION PRAYER(S)

S. Dominus vobiscum.
M. Et cum spiritu tuo.
S. Oremus.

Da nobis, quaesumus, Domine, Deus noster: ut, qui Nativitatem Domini nostri Jesu Christi mysteriis nos frequentare gaudemus; dignis conversationibus ad eius mereamur pervenire consortium: Qui tecum . . .

M. Amen.

P. The Lord be with you.
S. And with thy spirit.
P. Let us pray.

Grant us, we beseech Thee, O Lord our God, that we who rejoice in celebrating by these mysteries the birth of Our Lord Jesus Christ, may deserve by a worthy way of life to arrive at fellowship with Him: who liveth and reigneth with Thee . . .

S. Amen.

Post-Communion. The earliest character of this prayer, as known in the East, was that of a thanksgiving for Communion to conclude this section of the Mass, as Collect and Secret conclude Entrance and Offertory; Post-Communions, though fashioned in the Roman liturgy as petitions (on the model of Collect and Secret), are very rarely of a general character and keep a close connection with the idea of Holy Communion. As mentioned above, the *Quod ore sumpsimus* and the *Corpus tuum Domine* are old examples of this prayer.

CONCLUSION

S. Dominus vobiscum.
M. Et cum spiritu tuo.
S. Ite missa est *or* Benedicamus Domino.
M. Deo gratias.

P. The Lord be with you.
S. And with thy spirit.
P. Go, the Mass is ended, *or* Let us bless the Lord.
S. Thanks be to God.

[*at Masses for the dead*

S. Requiescant in pace.
M. Amen.

P. May they rest in peace.
S. Amen.]

Placeat tibi, sancta Trinitas, obsequium servitutis meae: et praesta: ut sacrificium, quod oculis tuae Majestatis indignus obtuli, tibi sit acceptabile, mihique, et omnibus pro quibus illud obtuli, sit, te miserante, propitiabile. Per Christum Dominum nostrum. Amen.

Let the performance of my homage be pleasing to Thee, O holy Trinity; and grant that the sacrifice which I, though unworthy, have offered up in the sight of Thy Majesty, may be acceptable to Thee, and through Thy mercy be a propitiation for me, and all those for whom it has been offered. Through, etc. Amen.

Benedicat vos omnipotens Dĕus, Pater et Filius et Spiritus sanctus.
M. Amen.

May God almighty bless you, Father, and Son and Holy Ghost.
S. Amen.

Concluding Blessing. By the middle of the fourth century it seems to have been an established practice in both East and West to end Mass with a prayer for a blessing and some sort of final blessing.[1] The "prayer for the blessing" is the variable *oratio super populum* (prayer over the people) which still occurs in our missal in the ferial Masses of Lent. Once there had been such a prayer proper to every Mass, like the Collect, etc., but the restriction of it to Lent had occurred by the end of the sixth century. It must, therefore, always have had some connection with penance and penitential seasons: it does not occur even now in the Sundays of Lent; and the introduction of it by *Humiliate capita vestra Deo* ("Bow down your heads to God") also wears a penitential aspect. It is suggested that once it was a blessing for the public penitents who were not receiving Communion—in place of Communion

[1] In Jerusalem at this date everyone went up to the bishop to be touched on the face at the end of Mass.

Post-Communion

Ite Missa est

Placeat . . .

The Blessing

—but with the invention of Lent in the fourth century came to be used only then and as a prayer over everyone (*super populum*), as Lent is a time of penance for all.

It seems odd that the Roman dismissal, *Ite Missa est* (literally, "Go, this is the dismissal") should wear such a secular air—being a formula similar to those in use for closing ordinary public meetings—while the Eastern rites have something more Christian.[1] But in fact *Missa* had come to be so regular a name for the Mass, that in Christian minds the word would have denoted the Mass or "the blessing at the end of Mass". (We find the word *missa*, literally "the dismissal of a gathering", being used in pagan Latin for "a gathering"; taken over by the Church, both *missa* and *collecta* were rough translations of the Greek *ecclesia*, *synagoge* or *synaxis*, and were used both for the gathering of the faithful for the Eucharist and for the dismissal-blessing at the end of it.) The omission of the real dismissal, *Ite Missa est*, and its substitution by *Benedicamus Domino* ("Let us bless the Lord") or *Requiescant in pace* ("May they rest in peace"), on days when there is no *Gloria*, probably derive from occasions when something was to follow, and therefore a dismissal was inappropriate—e.g. the continuation of the Office on weekdays; Vespers on Sundays in Lent; the Absolution and Burial after a *Requiem*.

The blessing itself is a formula of words (bene-*diction*) rather than an action. The Mass-books do not give any formula for a priest's blessing until this blessing came to be regarded as part of the Mass (and not something done on the way out) and our present blessing-formulas are from the thirteenth century. The Sign of the Cross is, of course, itself a most ancient Christian usage, but it was for long a signing of oneself. Any general custom of at any rate priests tracing a cross in the air when blessing other people seems to date from about the

[1] *Procedamus in pace: In nomine Christi, Amen,* eventually borrowed by the West for starting liturgical processions, e.g. on Palm Sunday.

tenth century, though it is in the nature of things rather hard to get any certain evidence for such a thing.

LAST GOSPEL

He goes to the Gospel side of the altar, and there he says

S. Dominus vobiscum.

M. Et cum spiritu tuo.

S. Initium sancti Evangelii secundum Joannem.

M. Gloria tibi, Domine.

In principio erat Verbum, et Verbum erat apud Deum, . . . (*John i. 1–14*).

P. The Lord be with you.

S. And with thy spirit.

P. The beginning of the holy Gospel according to John.

S. Glory to Thee, O Lord.

In the beginning was the Word, and the Word was with God, . . .

(at the end)

M. Deo gratias.

S. Thanks be to God.

Last Gospel. It will be remembered that at first only a bishop blessed the people at the end of Mass. For a long time, even when priests were regularly giving this blessing, a distinction was made in that priests blessed not with their hands but with objects—a crucifix, the corporal, paten, chalice. . . .[1] Among the objects used in the Middle Ages in Gallican lands was the Prologue of St. John's Gospel, written out by itself on a scroll. The great devotion to this Prologue[2] led to its being used on all sorts of occasions, and it was probably regarded as standing for the whole Gospel—as the Gospel Book itself would be an appropriate but difficult thing to bless with. The *reading* of this Prologue, as well, at the end of Mass first appears in the Dominican *Ordo* of 1256 and it is generally regarded as a praiseworthy custom by the end of the fifteenth century, though still not a usual practice in Rome itself till the missal of Pius V in the sixteenth. Other portions of the Gospels were sometimes read instead, and this developed into the practice of commemorating a concurrent feast by reading its Gospel in this place; this was enforced by Pius V and further

[1] A difference was also made in the words used, and still is, the bishop's blessing being prefaced by *Sit nomen Domini*, etc.

[2] See p. 54.

The Last Gospel

Benedicite servi Domini Domino . . .

regulated by Benedict XV in 1920 to the commemoration of all Masses which have their own proper Gospel. The reading of the Last Gospel soon lost its character of a blessing, and was given the opening formulas of the Gospel proper, *Dominus vobiscum* . . . *Initium sancti evangelii* . . . But a relic of this blessing character remains in the final response, *Deo gratias*.

Appendix I—THE PROPERS

THE Proper of any Mass (the part which varies from Mass to Mass) comprises Introit, Collect, Epistle, Gradual and Alleluia or Tract (Sequence), Gospel, Offertory chant, Secret prayer, Communion chant and Post-Communion prayer: i.e., there are three elements—the chants, the lections and the formal prayers.

The Propers for great feasts are composed of passages which are relevant to the occasion, giving the biblical account of the feast or expressing the religious ideas which it evokes; and there is nothing more of a quite general nature that needs to be said about them.

But Sundays and those weekdays which have their own Masses suggest no particular ideas of themselves, except in so far as they fall within one of the great periods of the Church's liturgical year—e.g. Advent, Paschal time. The Sunday Masses show in their lections a certain progression through the New Testament (and through the Book of Psalms in their chants[1]), in order to cover the whole of it as far as possible. Roughly speaking the progression is as follows:

Christmastide and Eastertide:	Relevant historical passages for both Epistles and Gospels.
Easter to Pentecost:	Epistles—Catholic Epistles.
	Gospels—John.
Pentecost to Advent:	Epistles—End of Catholic Epistles, then Paul's Epistles.
	Gospels—Latter half of Matthew, Mark and Luke.
Epiphany to Septuagesima:	Epistles—Rest of Paul's Epistles.
	Gospels—First half of Matthew, Mark and Luke.

[1] See pp. 69, 91, 175.

Pope Gregory I, at the end of the sixth century, revised the Roman missal, but there are good reasons for thinking that he left untouched the Masses of the Sundays after Pentecost and that these are of fourth- and fifth-century composition. They do not show in their prayers the very severe and almost colour-less characteristics of his revision, but are more florid and more lively. And there are other indications—for example, the Introit for the Tuesday after Pentecost is from the Fourth Book of Esdras;[1] St. Ambrose was one of the last people to defend the canonicity of this book, and at the formulation of the Canon of Scripture by Damasus I at the end of the fourth century it was excluded. The Epistles of these Masses after Pentecost show a regular progression through the Epistles of St. Paul. The Gospels are all from SS. Matthew, Mark and Luke, and thereby show some trace of the originally continuous course of reading through the Gospel, but they go backwards and forwards through the latter parts of these evangelists apparently without any principle. In some cases the Gospel seems to have been chosen to fit the Epistle—as on the seventh Sunday after Pente-cost, when the theme of both lections is that of "bearing good fruit". In other cases the choice of Gospel seems to be deter-mined by the proximity of the feast of some saint particularly venerated at Rome—e.g. the miraculous draught of fishes is recounted on the fourth Sunday, about the time of the feasts of SS. Peter and Paul (June 29); the Wise Steward comes on the eighth Sunday, near the feast of St. Lawrence (August 10); the healing of the paralytic is told on the eighteenth Sunday, about the time of the feast of SS. Cosmas and Damian (September 27), who were doctors.

Some of the puzzles about Sunday Masses seem to be due to the fact that chants, lections and prayers were originally con-tained in separate books, so that one section (e.g. the chants)

---

[1] " Eternal rest give unto them, O Lord, and let a perpetual light shine upon them " (Requiem Mass) is from the same source, as is the Alleluia chant on Christmas Eve.

could be rearranged without reference to the others, and any original theme running through a Mass would be thereby lost. There are some cases of Masses apparently being put together from the wrong parts, when copied into a single book—e.g. the second Sunday after Easter is Good Shepherd Sunday, and Epistle and Gospel both fit the one theme; but the Collect has no relevance to this idea, whereas the Collect of the third Sunday would fit it admirably.

Gregory I gave his attention rather to the development of the stational liturgy, which had begun before his time and continued to develop into the eighth century. There were Masses to be composed for numerous weekday occasions when a *statio* took place,[1] and the clue to the composition of these Masses is nearly always to be found in the church where the *statio* took place—either in the history of the saint to whom it was dedicated, or in some topographical fact or local custom. From the few private houses in which Mass had first been celebrated in Rome there grew up, besides the Lateran (the Pope's own church), the great basilicas and a number of smaller stational churches—exactly like the outlying parishes we find in a great cathedral city.[2] At first only known by titles of purely topographical import, or called after the donor of the house, they came to be dedicated to various saints whose relics were often laid in their respective churches as the cult of the martyrs grew in the fifth and subsequent centuries. From the welter of information about those among these churches where the stational Mass was held we may select a few items which will give an idea of how Masses are explained by the church for which they were composed.

On the Thursday after Ash Wednesday the *statio* is at the church of St. George, the soldiers' patron and himself a centurion in the Roman army according to the accounts of him.

[1] See p. 12.
[2] The feast of the consecration of a church is a feast of Christ and hence it is given great importance in the calendar.

So in the Gospel of that day we get the story of the centurion and Our Lord; the Epistle tells of the granting of life to the warrior-king Ezekias, and ends with words which are full of meaning if we imagine ourselves living in a Rome of the sixth century beset by enemies: "And I will deliver thee and this city out of the hands of the king of the Assyrians, and I will protect it" (Isa. xxxviii. 6).

On the Thursday after the first Sunday of Lent the *statio* is at "St. Lawrence in Panisperna"; according to tradition this was the site of his martyrdom on a gridiron, and the Introit is from the Mass of his feast. "In Panisperna" is a topographical designation and the origin of it is obscure, but it means simply "Bread and Ham": the compiler of Mass was clearly thinking of bread in his choice of both Gospel and Epistle and the verse for the Communion chant.

The theme of Rome's enemies encompassing her—the waves of Gothic tribes which swarmed into Italy when the Roman Empire collapsed—accounts for much in these stational Masses. Septuagesima Sunday's Mass begins "The sorrows of death surrounded me, and the torrents of iniquity troubled me . . ." (Ps. xvii. 5); the ideas are suggested as much by Rome's wars as by thoughts of the coming penitential season: for the stational Masses of these three Sundays before Lent were established at churches *outside the walls* of Rome, during a respite from the Lombard invasions when it was safe to go out of the city in procession. Septuagesima is at "St. Lawrence outside the Walls"; Sexagesima is at St. Paul's (it mentions him in the Collect) and its Gospel, the parable of the Sower, comes aptly at a time of year when sowing could be done peacefully in the outlying country; its Epistle gives Paul's own account of his sufferings and visions. Quinquagesima is at St. Peter's.

SS. Cosmas and Damian were famous doctors in Christian tradition, and their church, to which their bodies were carried, was a converted pagan temple dedicated to the Sacred City of

Rome; it became a healing-shrine, particularly for cases of fever, and hence we get the Gospel of Our Lord curing St. Peter's mother-in-law from fever, when the *statio* is celebrated there on Thursday after the third Sunday of Lent. If one reads the Epistle (Jer. vii. 1–7), one sees at once the reference to the conversion of a pagan temple into a Christian church—"I will dwell with you in this place . . . the temple of the Lord, the temple of *the Lord* . . ." The Collect of this Mass is the only other one besides that of Sexagesima to mention the patrons of the stational church. These two saints have their own feast (September 27), and the Introit of their feast's Mass, "Let the people show forth their wisdom . . ." (Ecclus. xliv. 15), and its Gospel (Luke vi. 17–23) recounting Our Lord's cures, have been taken over for the Common Mass used for the feasts of many martyrs (as by no means all saints have their own Mass), in spite of the fact that neither is very suitable to any other martyrs but these two "wise" doctors.

In the same way the Introit for the feast of St. Catherine of Alexandria (November 25), "I spoke of thy testimonies before kings" (Ps. cxviii. 46), which fits the story of her life, has been taken over for the Common of Virgin Martyrs, although it has no particular relevance to other virgin martyrs.

St. Cecilia is an interesting example, and must be our last. At the church dedicated to her the *statio* was held on Wednesday after the second Sunday of Lent, and she seems to have been the lady who originally owned the house. The Gospel tells us of the request of the mother of SS. James and John for them to sit on the right and left of Our Lord in His kingdom, and of His answer that they would indeed "drink the chalice", but that to sit on right and left was for the Father to allot. The explanation of this is that two other martyrs, Tiburtius and Valerianus, who shared her martyrdom and "drank the chalice" with her, were venerated at the same church with Cecilia; a ninth century mosaic shows them beside Cecilia as she is crowned, and it may well have replaced an earlier representation of the two martyrs on her right hand and on her left hand. Cecilia was a protector of Rome and the Epistle for this stational Mass gives us the prayer of Mardochaeus for the protection of his people—"have mercy on Thy people because our enemies resolve to destroy us . . ."—a prayer answered by Esther, a type of the Christian saint. The making of Cecilia into a patron of music is a misunderstanding of an antiphon in her Office, taken from the account of her life, *cantantibus organis Cecilia Domino decantabat*, which means that while the *pagans* played their instruments (the word can mean "organs") Cecilia sang hymns to God. The Epistle from Cecilia's feast day (November 22), "Thou hast exalted my dwelling place upon the earth . . ." (Ecclus. li. 13–17), has been taken over for the Common of Virgin Martyrs, though it was chosen for her because she gave her house to be a church.

Appendix II—CHRONOLOGICAL TABLE

Section	Mass Prayers	Primitive	Fourth Cent.	Fifth Cent.	Sixth Cent.	Seventh Cent.	Early Middle Ages	Later Middle Ages	Sixteenth Cent.
ENTRANCE	Iudica, etc.								Iudica
	Introit			Introit					
	Kyrie				Kyrie				
	Gloria			Gloria					
	Collect		Collect						
SYNAXIS	Epistle	Epistle							
	Gradual, etc.	Gradual							
	Sequence							Sequence	
	Munda cor meum							Munda cor meum	
	Gospel	Gospel							
	Sermon	Sermon							
	Creed						Creed		
OFFERTORY	Dom. vobiscum		Dom. vobiscum						
	Offertory chant			Offertory chant					
	Suscipe, etc.							Suscipe, etc.	
	Lavabo							Lavabo	
	Susc. sancta T.							Suscipe sancta T.	
	Orate fratres							Orate fratres	
	Secret		Secret						
EUCHARISTIC PRAYER	Preface	Preface							
	Sanctus		Sanctus						
	Benedictus				Benedictus				
	Te igitur					Te igitur			
	Memento					Memento			
	Communicantes					Communicantes			
	Hanc igitur				Hanc igitur				
	Quam oblationem				Quam oblationem				
	Qui pridie	Qui pridie							
	Unde et memores	Unde et memores							
	Supra quae		Supra quae						
	Supplices		Supplices						
	Memento etiam			(at Requiems only)			Memento etiam		
	Nobis quoque						Nobis quoque		
	Per quem						Per quem		
	Per ipsum—Amen	Per ipsum—Amen							
	Pater			Pater					
	Libera			Libera					
	Pax Domini	Pax Domini							
	Haec commixtio						Haec commixtio		
	Agnus Dei					Agnus Dei			
COMMUNION	Dne.J.C. qui							D.J.C. qui	
	Dne.J.C. Fili							D.J.C. Fili	
	Perceptio							Perceptio	
	Panem coelestem							Panem c.	
	Domine... dignus							Dne.n.s.d.	
	Corpus Domini	(similar form)						Corp. Dni.	
	Quid retribuam							Quid ret.	
	Sanguis Domini							Sanguis	
	Quod ore							Quod ore	
	Corpus tuum							Corp. tm.	
	Comm. chant				Communion chant				
	Post-Communion		Post-Communion						
CONCLUSION	Ite Missa est		Ite Missa est						
	Placeat						Placeat		
	Benedicat	(Blessing)						Benedicat	
	Last Gospel							Last Gosp.	

The beginning of a word gives a rough date for the prayer's insertion into the Roman liturgy.

Previous dots indicate either that the insertion may have been earlier, or that the prayer was in optional use before this time.